Life's Serenity

Edited by Heather Killingray

forwardpress

First published in Great Britain in 2009 by:
Forward Press Ltd.
Remus House
Coltsfoot Drive
Peterborough
PE2 9JX
Telephone: 01733 890099
Website: www.forwardpress.co.uk

SB ISBN 978-1 84418 481 1

Foreword

Although we are a nation of poets we are accused of not reading poetry, or buying poetry books. After many years of listening to the incessant gripes of poetry publishers, I can only assume that the books they publish, in general, are books that most people do not want to read.

Poetry should not be obscure, introverted, and as cryptic as a crossword puzzle: it is the poet's duty to reach out and embrace the world.

The world owes the poet nothing and we should not be expected to dig and delve into a rambling discourse searching for some inner meaning.

The reason we write poetry (and almost all of us do) is because we want to communicate: an ideal; an idea; or a specific feeling. Poetry is as essential in communication, as a letter; a radio; a telephone, and the main criterion for selecting the poems in this anthology is very simple: they communicate.

Contents

The Poems

The Night Watch

Looking down onto the deserted shore
To where lost souls of stranded seaweeds cling.
To pools where orphaned crabs patiently wait
For the returning tide to take them home.

The winter's daylight soon begins to fade
And quickening currents flood the bay
Rampaging through every creek and cove,
Scouring out each minute crack and crevice.

Rain-filled winds sweep across the cliffs
To whip the night-wrapped land into life.
Quivering trees bend low their leafless boughs
As the High Priest of Storms goes riding by.

Swift forks of flame stab darkening skies
And the cannon roar of thunder assails
The air with sounds of battle echoing
Through the shuttered streets of distant towns.

The sea, in one last frenzied endeavour,
Now hurls itself at the hated face of land
Until, wild-eyed and panting, it collapses
Like a beaten hound, silent and sullen.

As witness to these moments of madness
I watch the storm recover its sobriety
And watch the sea then rock itself to sleep
With dreams of encounters yet to be won.

Between the broken clouds I softly smile
At this foolishness. Yet, in my half-lit
I ifetime, of orbiting through time and space
I yearn for the ecstasy of your Earth.

John Eccles

Wind

Wind can be gales, wind can be breeze
Wind can chill water: making it freeze.
Cover mountains with just one sweep
Envelop the universe without a bleep
Winds can howl and winds can shriek
Wild undertones that can make you freak
Move through landscape, at any speed
Nature's way of stripping leaves and planting seed
Ruffles birds' feathers, blows the glittering snow
A thousand winds in God's hands; He controls the blow
Wind can stretch cobwebs; make them shiver
Wind is a taker; also a giver
Winds can be warm, embracing and cool
Or icy, cutting and cruel!
The wind travels in currents of air
Blows the rippling stream - invisible there.
Hurricanes, tornadoes caused by wind
This mighty, untamed force as yet to be pinned.

Vera Tyrer Collins

The Singing Sea Wind

The island Neanderthal rock paths
Left to guiltless nature
As in antiquity, sent to cut the cloth of gold
As Vikings hunting in the water world
In their domain starved of justice
As their tricks and ragged appearance
Blinded, crushed with distorted vengeance
They would oscillate the land
As a fervent glow, as memory
Then with clerics cloth overpowered
The mysterious voices are at last subdued
The Camelot clouds of night
Broke away to the glittering morning
Through the foggy mountain tops.

Edward Tanguy

Nature In The Garden

The lawn is cut and very neat -
A joy to see such sward;
But, look, a plantain's growing there
And cannot be ignored.

The roses climb in glorious blooms
Up to the cottage eaves,
But look more closely and you'll see
The black spot on the leaves.

Begonias spread their bright array -
They surely can't hold evil?
Alas, they're suffering an attack
Of a malicious weevil.

Grow all your lovely vegetables
If you for greens will hanker,
But keep alert in case you spot
The dreaded turnip canker.

Thrips menace your chrysanths and peas
And wire worms eat your spuds,
The woolly aphid tastes your fruit
Blackcurrants get big buds.

Eelworms like narcissus bulbs
Warmth thrills the spider mite,
Clematis wilt and collar rot
Attack your flowers in spite.

And in the greenhouse you will find
That horrid mealy bug,
And eating all your lettuces,
A greedy gourmet slug.

Yet gardeners play this unfair game -
Still join the endless fight
With coddling moth and ink disease
And every form of blight.

Barbara Jefferies

Life's Seasons

It's springtime
Life awakens underground
Sap is rising, buds are bursting
Freshness all around.

A new birth
A tiny babe begins its life
Big eyes watching, hands exploring
Innocent of strife.

It's summertime
Flowers bloom in colours bright
Sun is shining, showers are fleeting
Even warm the night.

Now grown up
Come and gone the flush of youth
Life's exciting, scheming, planning
Ever seeking truth.

Now autumn's here
Trees decide it's time to rest
Fruits are ripening, leaves are falling
Colour's at its best.

Reached middle-age
Experienced and earthly-wise
Families growing, home-nests leaving
Cutting apron ties.

It's wintertime
Mother Nature's gone to sleep
White the landscape, crisp cold gripping
Creation's secrets keep.

Old age beckons
Memories now the passing years
Oh so sleepy, tired, exhausted
No more time for tears.

Seasons come and go
Life begins and then grows old
Never-ceasing generations
Precious as gold.

Margaret Worsley

Year Of The Eternal Spring

Criss-cross hemispheres
Chase the sun the
Golden glow into which the
Nose accelerates to
The speed of sound
Whistling over the ground its
Shadow passing by in an instant
Across the fertile soil and
The fresh, green shoots

Spinning nature on its head
The Earth on its axis
Whirling madly the
Golden sun held
Suspended in
The palm of my hand
Frozen, a fiery ball of ice

And then swirling back the
Other way
Shadows recede back
Inside my shoes
Back across the still, imaginary
Line
Floating through time
Living, yet unconscious -

Calm and accepting, at peace
Resting in the land
Of falling gold.

Michael Durrant

Landscape

Ripples across the lake
Movement to the edge
Slow, careful as the
Searching mind.
Trees firm and still
Reaching into creation
Verdant branches reach
Like longing for truth
Breeze touches my face
A gathering hand.

Now, this landscape
This lake mirroring
Have a sense of a child
With enquiring eyes.
Birds, cattle, horses, sheep
Nurture the child among them
They gather the child
To themselves as I now
Gather with the reverence
Of my wakened gathering eyes.

George Coombs

March Madness

The cutting wind tore down the alley
Shovelling leaves and butts in its wake
Whisking her hair to a froth and a frenzy
Waterfall eyes merging into a lake.

It followed its course over walnut whip potholes
Zigzag reflections in watery haze
Over cool cobbles small mounds of resistance
To the wide open space and the end of its days.

Gaelyn Jolliffe

A Walk At Twilight

(In the shadows of Sliabh Gullion Mountain, Moyola River, a reflection on where my home and family live called The Hill)

Treading the wild fields
Along the riverbank
Sunset recedes and Gullion shields
Golden rays from the dark
Dewy carpet falling on Moyola
Valley from the hill beyond.

Returning by moonlight to retrace
My steps in the creeping shadows
Of the trees and waters ripple and race
Over gravel stones through the meadows
Small trees and hedgerows
In the vale below
From 'The Hill' beyond.

Now wending my way
By the pathway near the railway
I proceed towards my home on the hill
Whose lights I perceive to appear
Lighting my haven on 'The Hill' beyond.

D J Barton

Hymn To Spring

Spring has come once again to this land that we love
Proud trees raise their arms to the clear skies above
Daffodils golden heads lifting towards the sun
Reincarnation of dead earth, new life begun
Within the heart a new stirring of the blood.
After the cold of winter, life again feels good
There's so much to behold, to make one hold one's breath
That with all things being reborn, it's hard to think of death
Yet all things must die, to once again be born
As sure as after the dark night, comes the new day's dawn.

Gwladys Mills

The End Of The Spring

Could it be with
All the tempests that rack the Earth
And the greenhouse
Effect
That soon
There will be no spring
And all seasons will be one?
Spring only to be celebrated in the
Flowers
That speak of it
Who their life cycles
Synchronise
With the new age of no winter
And no spring
That is our future
That speaks to us from the world without
And speaks of other things
Other times

Where seasons will be as one
Weather, little different
In the advanced greenhouse stage
And the signs of spring will be gone
With just a long unending summer.

Alasdair Sclater

Sprout

Days are passing
Leaves are falling
Whatever event that records
If it states as spirit
Gains a new mode of living
Spring composes new springing
Takes a form of nature flow
For flowering new evolution.

Bollimuntha Venkata Ramana Rao

Mawley Oak

The ancient oak has fallen, fallen
Lies shattered and splintered torn apart
Centuries have passed beneath its boughs
The forest whispered, shuddered at its loss
Now its death shroud is the soft green moss
It stood resplendent in winter's frost
Bare boughs black against a clear blue sky
Tinted pink and red by day's first blush
In summer's breeze, its leaves would dance and sing
In harmony with the sparkling stream
And echoing birdsong arias
Filled its emerald-green canopy

The ancient oak has fallen, fallen
Wide its girth that grew through centuries
Each broken bough, big as any tree
Its shadow will never fall again
Taken back by night's dark cold embrace
Now it's shattered, splintered, stretched out corpse
Is brushed by the raven's passing shadow
Is bridged by the rainbow's fleeting arch.

David Walford

The Power Of The Planet Of The Seas

The seas are mighty, the seas are deep
They are always in motion and never sleep
The seas are active and they are blue-green
They defy any man-made machine
They quench the magma beneath them too
Making many islands, which are hazardous to view
The seas are lovely
But, they can bring death
We can drown in them
As they snatch our last breath.

Peter John Morey

Symphony To Summer

As the garden starts to rise
From her night's rest
The sight before your eyes
A wondrous surprise
Giving us her very best
Heady perfume everywhere
Cobwebs like gossamer lace
Butterflies in such haste
Roses in full bloom
Sweet peas - dahlias and lupins
All around you
Pass through the archway
Entwined with honeysuckle
To the lily pond
'Sparkling new'
As the sun breaks through
Pansies in beds
And old Tom's shed
See, the watering can's been left out
And near the wishing well
A gravel path
Leading to the summerhouse
A place to rest
In Nature's bounty.

Margaret Parnell

Spring Reborn

Winter rolls away at last
Freedom from its icy blast:
Snow and hail shall disappear
Silent nights and darkness drear.

Spring begins to show her face
All the wonders of her grace
From the earth come new green shoots
Firmly held by deep strong roots.

Brighter skies and longer days
Join together with sun's haze
Flowers of every hue are seen
Mingled with all shades of green.

Nesting birds with joy do sing
Bearing twigs upon the wing
Seeing neither friend nor foe
Back and forwards they do go.

Tiny lambs adorn the green
Gambling round they set the scene
Fluffy chicks rush about
Yellow balls for spring to shout.

Let the little signs give cheer
Greet this brightest time of year
Seize the hour and use it well
Till the days of summer swell.

Margaret Nixon

Global Warming

Flowers are blooming that should be long dead
Birds swoop on crusts to fill their beak and mouth
The warmth has our seasons all stood on their head
There's birds still around here that should have flown south.

To cut down on fossil fuels, big powers refuse
CO_2 has made holes in our poor ozone layer
We need a renewable power source to use
Survival now hangs on a wing and a prayer.

Atomic power stations are the answer, it would seem
They'll supply all our power and fill all our needs
But hippie protesters all wave signs and scream
Such power, they say, will sow cancerous seeds.

So the weather gets warm and the polar caps melt
The oceans all rise and devour the lands
We blame everybody who burns oil or coal
Unable to see that it's in our own hands.

Mick Nash

Spring Brings More Fun

Spring has come
Daffodils welcome the sun
Standing proud and tall
Providing a colourful picture for us all.

The lighter nights make us smile
We have been left in the dark for such a long while
As daylight increases each day
We feel naturally brighter and want to play.

Day trips can last longer
Recharged we feel stronger
Knowing soon summer will be here
Brings lots of happy thoughts and much cheer.

Julie Marie Laura Shearing

Hi-Tech 2008

Today we're very hi-tech and everything's on line -
Everyone sends emails for it saves a lot of time.
Computers are a way of life - it's not about the cost;
There's so much info on the web - without one you'll be lost.

The world's so complicated - just don't forget your PIN;
The Lottery's taken over - it's a £1 a go to win.
Cash is 'out' and cheques are too - for paper's not in fashion -
And booking on the internet is this generation's passion.

If looking for employment, you must be up to speed
With the latest programmes, data, software that they need.
And people now have iPods or get an MP3
Or buy huge plasma screens - but it's just a large TV.

The news is full of doom and gloom; plus violence, sickness, crime;
Jesus is our only hope; accept Him while there's time.
The world is out of our control; and Heaven a breath away -
But after death, no turning back - so call on God today.

For life on Earth is temporary, and nothing here will last,
So take the hand of Jesus now and He'll forget your past.
He'll accept you with His loving arms, there'll be no code or key,
For Jesus died for everyone - and He'll welcome you or me.

For my eternal home's not here; instead I'm Heaven-bound -
No fear of death in this life, for with Jesus I'll be found.
And I know my Heavenly Father will not ask me for my PIN,
Or ask me for my password, for He saved me from my sin.

No 'option one, two, three or four' and no 'access denied'
For the Lord loves each one dearly, and for everyone He died.
You won't be asked for details, for your ID or your name,
For Jesus knows them anyway and He loves you just the same.

Don't rely on earthly things, for they'll all pass away;
But put your trust in Jesus, who will come again one day;
For He'll judge the living and the dead; and every knee will bow -
Don't delay in accepting Jesus as your Saviour - act right now!

Susan King

Nature Through The Psychedelic Lens

Green greenery
Scenic scenery
The smell of fresh cut grass
As you walk on past
Folds of rolling hills
In the distance spills

In the graveyard
A pheasant roams
Amongst the graveyard stones
Not making a sound -
- not wanting to be
Discovered and found

And rebellious flowers
Rusty old daffodils
Pansies and snowdrop crops
Rise up in swathes
Covering the graves

Fields of acid yellow
Steal my eyes, squinting
In a hazy daze, glinting
All calm and mellow

And beyond, up to the skyline
Poppy flowers lend their magic powers
Drowning the hills in a fine red wine
And wind wrapped snowy showers
Of white blossom flowers decline

A secret stash of bluebells
As if forbidden - don't tell
Beyond the bracken, lie hidden
And unwell, losing their potent colour
Becoming duller and slacken

The river lazily
Lackadaisically pulls
Itself along, languorous
Slow and sluggish
Heavy and lethargic
Although the stream
Rapidly rushes on

And the sun now drowsy
And dozy drops down
Its head

Into the psychedelic bed
Of the evening sky
Split and slit open
In gashes, slashes
And colour clashes
Of oranges, pinks and reds

Jane Air

Spring

The smell of fresh cut grass
I can't believe spring's here at last

Running round in the midday sun
Me and my friends, having so much fun

Flowers blooming everywhere
Catching the sun in the garden chair

We're all so happy, spring's here at last
Ever so glad winter went so fast.

Stacey Wreford (12)

Tropical Spring/Sea Flying

Countless islands scattered on a turquoise sea
Like a fragmented flag of universal love
Each striped with white sand, blue sea
Each brightening with the fresh lime green
Of new leaves, nodding in an onshore breeze.
Even though we have no dancing daffodils
No gusts of bluebell music through the woods
We have the hot-pink, orange and scarlet
Of bougainvillea, the exotic stippled shades
Of showy orchids bowing, swaying to our gaze
And out on the sea, climbing to the meniscus of the world
We are blown along on a newly spring, spring wind
On slender barques of painted, carved wood
Barely held to the sea by outriggers of curved bamboo
As frail as water boatmen on English ponds. It seems
As if we could fly, way into the sky, if the butterfly wings
Of bright sail were not held back on ropes in the brown hands
Of the boatmen, gently reining in the bounding yacht
As we lie back above the ocean over the outriggers,
The only sound as of tearing silk as the boat slips through the sea.
Small waves leap and slap our rumps, spangles blind us
The sinking sun torches the sand and sea on its path
And this is as close to Heaven as we will ever get.

Liz Davies

Still Life

A shell, small, insignificant
Placed on a table in an artist's studio
With driftwood, seaweed and a lobster claw;
Though far removed from where you should belong
You still present your beauty to the eye.
Spirals and calcareous ripples mimic sea.
While shades of cream and umber hint at sand,
And in your hidden depths you carry song.

Joan Lund

Spring

I thought I had lost you
As I walked home with my head
Full of other people's thoughts and feelings -
Pettiness ranging from,
'I can't work Thursday's, I have a dog to look after'
To,
'I can't work Tuesday because the unit is being decorated,
You're the manager, you supervise it'
People with selfish aims, they take the Bank Holiday money and run
No regard to the thirty dementia sufferers we are there for.

And the sky was grey and overcast, a cold snowy Easter
Where was that sign of spring?
Where was that sign stating that the days are warming, lengthening?

Then I saw you, slender green shoot breaking through concrete
And I found hope again
For if you, delicate as you are, finds a way through cold stone
Then so can I . . .

Mark Marsh

Spring

Springtime is here
The daffs are all out
Tulips are swaying
Their heads all about
All different colours of ev'ry hue
Even the primrose is peeping through.

The birds are busy building their nests
Hoping their efforts will past the test -
For bringing up young ones from the very first start
Then learning to sing right from the heart.

Barbara Wickens

Spring

Dark brown soil
Freshly ploughed
Strong earthy smell
Fills my nostrils.

I kneel down
And sink my hands
Deep into the soft
Yielding earth.

Nature's food
Encouraging growth
Seeds to seedlings
Life springs forth.

After winter's dormancy
Life begins again
A new cycle
New beginnings.

Marie-Thérèse Ryan

Remorse

Remorse rotates in the void
With leaves withered
As well as memories scattered

Then falls from a funnel
Casts a million crusts
Of forests
As well as oceans

Uprightly concentrates
Within a second ceases
As if never
Then rotates on

David Lin

Spring In My Garden

I'm looking out the window
And spring is almost here
Our camellia's are showing off
The daffodil yellow shines clear.

The buds are popping in the copse
Making the shrubs more dense
We've blue tits in the nesting box
And the robin's on the fence.

The magpie's nest is occupied
The squirrel's on the feed
The air is fresh, the grass is green
What more do we need?

All the roses are budding up
The climber's standing tall
Suddenly the forsythia's out
And spring is on the ball.

Brian Hurll

Coastline

Far, as far as the eye can see
The sky and the oceans meet
Where the horizon draws a perfect line
Straight and complete.

On the heaving swell
White horses ride the waves
Until they smash against the sculptured cliffs
Or die on the glistening sands.

All along the coastline
This performance consistently goes
Since time began and until it ends
But when, nobody knows.

Leslie Frank Checkley

Autumn Then Winter

Leaves scattered, blow and turn
Into the vibrant colours we love
The wind like a brush
Gently sweeps them up
Tumbling them all around
The air so crisp
Sharp, ready to bite
Autumn winds, turning to winter
To meet Jack Frost's cold, cold toes
Scarves and gloves will be brought out
Children's warm laughter
Their shiny bright eyes
Snowmen with carrots as noses
And lopsided smiles
Glistening, white, bluey snow
Black skies with stars twinkling
Their luscious lights
Soon, will be Christmas
New comings
New life!

Evelyn Riverside

Spring

Spring green leaves
Dripping with rain
A fresh shower
Soaking the parched earth
Like a thirsty soul
It drinks up those precious drops
Fresh life
With new purpose
Destiny finding its course
Lives with a purpose
A scene of rebirths
A second chance
For another, it's all brand new
The first shot at life
However tremulous
Might turn up tremendous
Walking through the earth
Like a breathless shadow
Discovering creation
Seeking and finding the creator
All from a spray of rain
Through the span of spring.

Debra Ayis

Spring

New buds beginning to break forth.
Crocus and snowdrops emerging like a new breath
onto winter's tired earth.
Beads of colour, a kaleidoscope
forever switching and changing hue.
Spring is coming.

Clear skies replacing the dark grey dawn.
Blues of every shade and white scudding clouds
paint their pictures across the heavens.
Birds head back from warmer climes
to welcome the spring.

A warmer breeze drifting through trees
littered with new growth.
Sunlight's bright beams
rousing the fluttering dawn chorus;
And reaching through windows
to disturb children from their slumber
and wake them for breakfast.
Spring is here!

Tracy Somers

Life's Reflections

On muddy waters
Of ebbing tide
Sails
A golden sun
A view
A scene
And memories
Of youth
Of age
Of time.

S Brown

Winterfire

Bleached fossils
Polished in the rain swells
Gone the hot dry wind
And bohemian wayfarer
Such a man
Such a red-gold man
Charcoal roadbirds part then
Return in my wake to
Their wintry carrion stones
A heatless sun sets its marble coat
Upon my tangled hair
I must find more temperate climes
To stave off the whip
Of the next
Bruising
Winterfire.

Mokha Laget

The Hoary Old Willow

Slender branches trail the rough waters over which they hang
Like bony fingers creakingly caressing the waves
Ruffled by the spring gales
Turbulent waters chopping against the floral banks
While above lamb-like clouds swirl in Heaven's dance
Wind howls like hungry wolves
Foraging for food after the barrenness of winter
The slender branches overhead are clothed in green
Heralding the forthcoming of nature's bounteous gift
Clothing the barren boughs in gossamer green
Age-old he stands at the water's edge
Marking time from season to season
As accurate a calendar of nature's turning cycle
The hoary old willow.

Jane Dyson

The Hawthorn

I always know when spring has come
When I see the May in bloom
Its white flowers look like a mass of snow
Dispelling thoughts of winter's gloom.

The hawthorn gets its common name
Not from the haws born on the thorn
But from the Old English word haegthorn
Which defines its use as the hedge thorn.

Its leaves are favoured by horse and ox
Who would devour them to the ground
But for the sharp spines which protrude
From the older branches which abound.

When autumn comes tis then we see
The crimson haws born on the bushes
Food for the birds when winter comes
A feast for blackbirds and the thrushes.

David A Garside

Mother Earth

In spring when Earth begins to wake
My pleasure lies in England fair
Rising from darkness into light,
Transforming the soil with lacy patterns green
As plants leave their winter resting place
And shoots quietly appear.

Humans watchful for the sun, sing in their hearts for joy
As it travels ever higher, throwing energy into minds
And daylight on the walls,
Some other creatures of the planet leave their
Hibernation and search for food -
A most necessary presence.

Monica Redhead

Planet Of Dreams

Opportunity, a way to joyful free-scope
Right now, chance to catch your dream
Poised for release to the call of hope
The breakthrough, just a fleeting bright gleam.

Try action you had to suspend in delay
Towards the call to succeed with flair
Grasp the chance to find the way
With avoidance, swift the release of despair.

Important you progress, imagine all is well
Strong desire is the key to open the door
With much to offer, now break the spell
And find all you were long waiting for.

Fleeting the spur to grasp the chance
When history of confusion blocked with demand
Limited your scope of support to enhance
Emerge today, embrace the gift of vision and understand.

Betty Bukall

New Dawn

While out travelling in our car
I notice the early morning mist disappear over the hedgerow
We can see the cows standing still
Waiting for the sun to shine
My heart thrills at the sight of new lambs born
The sound of bleating, 'Where is Mum?'
Birds at first light begin to sing
And we know that nature is a wonderful thing
If we take care of the soil, flowers will bloom
Transforming the planet into a colourful wonderland
Contentment comes on silent air
We can see nature's beauty everywhere.

Joan M Waller

Aftershock
(2006 Earthquake in Asia)

Radio breaks it brusquely:
'Earthquake shatters homes -
Thousands killed or injured;
Snug in comfort zones

We hear measured tones
Number scale, name nations.
Between the sip and cup
Words drop like bombs -

Shatter, overwhelm us.
News rifts with death
At a distance: each pause
A last, stopped breath.

Outside, splashing red
A robin slight as breath
Alights, crams berries:
Feels itself at rest.

Shivering within, we reel
At Earth's cruel rock:
Feel shared ground shift
In far-off aftershock.

Rosemary Doman

A Weather Design

On a regular basis my wife says
The weather changes in many ways
If she puts washing on the line
One minute the sun will shine
Then it rains and clouds go dark
Even at the local park.

A tumble dryer I will go and buy
Just as long as the day is dry
Then spend more money drying clothes
Should I peg out? Nobody knows
So I'll send a postcard to my wife
She's upstairs experiencing life.

I tell my children the weather will change
A coat or a jacket I try to arrange
Taking them to school every day
I really would like the shining sun to stay
Yet again I ponder of getting rid of damp
So I will get up and switch on the bedroom lamp
Whatever time of the day it is
The weather nowadays is a huge miss
Be it needed on a summer's day
We will stay at home and play.

Lee Connor

The Creation Of Spring

Rejoice! Icy winds of winter are gone
The flowers once more appear on the earth
The snowdrops dance with white heads in the verge
Daffodils will show yellow trumpets
Beautiful hyacinths perfume our air
Making our gardens joyously pleasant
Tulips follow; we enjoy their colours
The trees are budding showing spring is here.

Feathery birds know their appointed time
We listen to their joyous notes
Collecting straw and grass to build their nests
Soon little babies will peer over their beds
And fly up to the boundless sky and clouds
Joining other flocks, delighting our eyes
As we watch them fly and whirl around
The frogs croak, ponds are ideal for their eggs
Which the fish love, so tadpoles are few.

The night sky darkens reaches into dawn
Spring Venus too reaches into the sky
As dawn fades and flows into Nature's morn
All nature is attune with joyous praise.

The blue sky, the ponds, the hedges, the fields
Teem yearly so we enjoy their pleasure
How majestic His boundless care
The moonlit sea is a path of beauty
Millions on Earth are cared for by God
Night sky above with billions of stars
The sun for warmth and growth and light daily
God always giving us His creation.

Alice Blackburn

Somewhere

This is a cruel and harsh, bleak place
The enemy rains and abrasive winds
Vying, constantly waging war, trying
To carve their names onto the rock face
Of old, hollowed crags; rugged with grime.
Weathered by the raw crust of time
Thrusting, they jut their jagged jaws' edge
In defiance against a blistering force
A bare, unyielding nature source
That seeks to destroy, pierce a wedge
Into the tor, granite-grey, splintering sky
At this height even eagle dare not fly
For fear his mighty wings be ripped
To plunge him flightless to the depths.

This landscape is not for the likes of man
Such a terrain was planet planned
Forever to be untamed, uncharted
Here, no venturing for the faint-hearted
But, eventually will come one to pace
Test their skills and willingness, to race;
Enduring the pulsing heart that senses
Finally, the summit will be turbulence
And by so doing, ignore the warning taunts
Of steel-challenging, forceful elements
That wield a power as rightful heirs
To defend the wilderness that is theirs.
So, with no firm foothold for ascent
Man's will is sliced and all is severance
Nature reclaims her inheritance to embrace
This is a cruel and harsh, bleak place.

Janine Vallor

The Price Of Freedom

Love, what's the price of freedom?
As when the ice packs melt, should it flood the Earth?
I hear they are hunting whale and elephant again
Everyone's worried about life on Mars
Hear the distant drums of wars, a distant strum
No one minds really, poo in the sea or factory
Billowing out acid rain
Or a world obsessed with millions of motorcars
Here is the price of freedom by the dollar and the pound
The Brazilian rainforest, the lungs of the Earth
A time for extinction and destruction of possible cure
A time to wonder how and why we lived
Not to take but to one day give
To express that sex and money are not the only importance
To save the Earth before it does die
For everyone from elderly to a baby that cries.

Barry Powell

It Covers Tracks

It covers tracks and shifts the desert sands
It cools the overheated brow and soothes the cheek
It fills the brightly coloured sails to billowing shapes
And sways the crops to seas of golden waves
It whips the water into frenzied foam
It carries high above a fragile paper shape
And lifts the smoke in swirling coiling whirls
It wafts the scents of garden blooms afar
And fans a flickering flame to furnace heat
It causes havoc with tremendous force
And dries the soaked earth to solid grains
It cools the blazing heat of tropic sun
And drives the rain across the parched terrain
It screeches and it whistles through the eaves
It wills the noon-day buzzes into sleep
And is a constant factor of our lives.

Nina Woolf

Beauty Of Life

I see great beauty in my life most every day
I see the sun arise, I see it go away
And every time it takes away my breath
To see the birth of light, to see its death.

To see the fragile beauty of a flower
The gentle feeling of a summer shower
The shining beauty of a bride in white
All these things bring pleasure to the sight.

To watch a baby, first begin to smile
To watch a deer pause its flight to rest awhile
The busy doings of a bumblebee
Life has a wondrous beauty, you can see.

So look and you will find there's beauty everywhere
As if sweet Mother Nature likes to share
You only have to pause and glance around
Yes, everywhere you look, it can be found.

Gordon Andrews

Nature's Firework Display

Over-ripe fruit on the apple trees
Oak leaves snatched by an autumn breeze
Within the forest the only sound
Are pine cones tumbling to the ground.
Where squirrels on branches overhead
Toss acorns onto a leafy bed
Russel-gold tones light up the days
As colours explode like firework displays
Autumn leads summer to a gentle close
Before winter strikes Earth into deep repose.
To slumber and sleep in an icy trance
Amid diamond frost as the snowflakes dance.
Then in the spring with hope reborn
The lark will soar in early morn
As the sun awakens a still quiet Earth
With the warm soft touch of miraculous rebirth.

Jean Mackenzie

Springtime

All nature come to life
Free from winter's strife
And we human beings
Watching and seeing.

Nature's activity
In towns and villages
Coming to life
All kinds of images.

Slow moving snails
With their silvery trails
All around the garden
Not begging pardon.

Beautiful butterflies
Settling on sweet peas
Carrying pollen
For flowers to increase.

Bees as well
From flower to flower
Sucking nectar
On each and every hour.

Ladybirds I also see
Flying around
Among flowers
That abound.

Francis Xavier Farrugia

Eden Revisited

Sweet the remembrance,
Heart of my father
Beating and in tune
With Nature's wildness;
His Garden Eden,
His life and of life,
His love and of love,
His tears and of tears.
This labour of love
Nurturing its growth
With a deep fervour
And such passion that
Eden is wholly
Of him, my father
And solely of me.
Thus, memories sweep
Overwhelming me . . .
A soothing fusion
Of scents and colour
Which lull the senses
To dream lazily,
Sensing hazily
My father's aura
Dwelling nigh in peace
And tranquillity
In His paradise,
And we speak, each one
To the other, when
In fragrant Eden.

Gwendoline Douglas

Spring Rhapsody

When the sun's high in the blue of the sky,
And the bright fields of grass light up with the dew:
We know that the season of spring must be nigh,
And the verges are filled with flowers of gold hue.

When the sheen of the coppery willow's ablaze,
And the babble of water of each little stream
Ripples across the white stones, while the haze
Of the sky enhances the silver-touched gleam.

When the pale yellow primroses light up the ditches,
And the daffodils trumpet the sound of the breeze:
We know that the world is full of God's riches,
Which are crowned by the glory of blossoming trees.

Magnolias proudly hold up their chalices,
And camellias beam each bright ruby face:
Both would adorn the most ornate of palaces,
While sweet cherry trees show off their pink lace.

After the showers the rainbow shines, shimmers
With glorious colours, I oft long to capture
That moment in spring when everything glimmers,
Thanks be to God for each springtime of rapture.

Janet Lang

Scorpions

Scorpions, scorpions, everywhere
They are as universal as humans
Some are found in rainforests and open plains
Some prefer sandy deserts and snow-topped hills.
In the tropics, they aestivate during drought
In the temperates, they hibernate during winter
What adaptable creatures!

Scorpions, scorpions, everywhere
They are as viviparous as humans
All nurture and protect their baby scorplings
All are prey to birds, reptiles and small mammals
During the night, they come out to hunt and feed
During the day, they hide in holes and under rocks
What vulnerable creatures!

Scorpions, scorpions, many kinds
All are equipped with the venomous tail
They are often harmless to healthy humans
They could be harmful to the young, old or sick
Some use their venoms just to subdue their prey
Some do have venoms as lethal as the cobra's
What remarkable creatures!

Eunice Ogunkoya

Where Has Winter Gone?

Where has winter gone?
All the brilliant fun
In the snowy, cold sun
Where has winter gone?
All it does now is rain
Again and again and again.
Where has winter gone
With its bright, sparkling frost
Are those crisp mornings lost
Where has winter gone?
With hats, scarves and gloves
And the sledding kids love
Where has winter gone
Will snowmen be a thing of the past
Can this warm weather really last?
Where has winter gone
There's daffodils out in Feb
And spiders in the web
Where has the winter gone
I bet it will be back soon!

Daphne Cornell

September Mornings

Mysterious, magic moments
Murky mist around
Carefully creeping through the forest
Hardly any sound

Spiders' webs dripping
From every bush and tree
Visible in the dewy mist
Enabling us to see
Translucent fragile patterns
Enormous and petite
So easily destroyed
In the daytime heat.

Silent, secret, special
Sunshine creeping through
Disappearing spiders' webs
No longer can we view.

The magic of the morning
Evaporating fast
But safe within our mind's eye
The magic will last and last.

Christine Hardemon

White Heather

White heather, white as snow
Oh how you do grow
With such a lovely glow
Always on show
First flower of the year
So much love so near
How quickly you appear
Like the snow
White as the morning bright
In the sun
You are such a delight
Just like Heaven's light
Like a dream in the night
A dream of love that comes true
It is so wonderful
To see you.

Gordon Forbes

A Summer's Day

There isn't anything I wouldn't do
For you
At the end of the rainbow
There's peace and harmony
Yes my love, I'll sing you a song
That won't take long

There's fresh heather I can smell
Just by the wishing well

There are bees and wasps
And oh, golly gosh, what a sting
Pollen and sunshine is what they want
So please don't worry
Don't dismay
It's lovely here on a happy sunny day.

Debbie Storey

Nostalgia

I should like to lie
with your lips tasting
the dedicated life of me
as once they did that summer
on a Grecian mountainside
warmed by the heat of lust and love,
a heavy brilliance
of mad mid-August sunshine
but yet I know
those days are gone
when we had time to spare.

So all things pass
and love is only one of them.
Yet, if we had sipped the juice
of that life then, not now,
we might have wandered on to
wilder, wider shores of exploration
and through the knowledge of
each other's lives reorganised our own
and lived with greater care.

In my solitude which is not lonely,
in my understanding of the truth
as I recognise it now
I know that chance is born but once,
a second chance is rare.

I smell anew the fragrance
of that mountainside
feel sunshine tender on my face
and see your lips hovering
over mine, ready to taste
not the life in me
but the waiting death.
I tell myself it isn't fair
yet it is still summer.

Isabel Cortan

The Fall

As leaves
Fall to the ground
Autumn
Is coming around
Squirrels prepare
Up and down
They are
Storing before snow
Birds can be seen
Barley the gleans
Golden grains
Filter forth
Mellowness
Can never be bought
Autumn her coat
Of many colours
Arrayed
Turning brown
Swinging, swinging
From above
A time of thankfulness
Beauty of leaves
To touch
Like a child
Ripple of laughter
As they fall
Preparing rebirth
Miracles that appear
Buds
Begin another year.

Maureen Thornton

Have You Seen?

Have you see
How the animals play?
What a wonderful thing
I'm feeling today.

Have you seen
The lightning strike?
But only for a sec
Oh what a delight.

Have you seen
The rain fall?
But hiding in your house
Not wanting to get wet at all.

Have you seen
The roaring sea?
So powerful
Makes me smile with glee.

All of these things
So beautiful and bright
But all of these things
Could be gone by tonight.

So as you sleep
Tucked up in bed
Put this thought
In your head.

You can make a difference
To global warming
It will affect you!

Abigail Webb

Annual Arrivals

Like sentries they stood in bright array
Guarding territory? Why were they there?
No one questioned, but genuinely admired
This annual even, crocuses is stripy attire.

Slender and sleek with yellow swaying heads
Opening shiny coats, revealing pearly seeds
Standing in black earth, tended with care
Flourishing with lots of fresh air.

A percentage of humans can relate to this state
Healthy environment, but surrounded by hate
Give a thought to those who minister care
To unfortunate folks, silent and scared.

Thankful we are, when given freedom space
Enjoying our lives, as we travel by God's grace
Giving Him full control, when another season arrives
Through nourishment from the Bible, our future will survive.

Annie Harcus

A Reptilian Scene

The jungle's still and dark and wide,
Where lie the snakeys, side by side;
Who dare approach, who dare advance
To see those eyes convey their trance?
There'll be a price, indeed there will
To get too close to that head so still;

The head will rise, the neck will snap,
In sinks the fangs, in deep the bite,
The teeth give forth of their vile sap
And the prey can struggle, but lose the fight;
The jungle's still and dark and cruel,
And danger lurks where the snakeys rule.

Alistair McLean

Global Warming?

Pale blossom unfurls on the tree in the sun
Fooling us to believe that spring has begun.
It's not so many winters gone
Puce clouds shed snow on everyone
And mallards skidded on frozen lake
To reach the bank our bread to take.
In the room at the top of my little house
Winter drove in the scurrying mouse
And frost drew patterns on windowpane,
A work of art in a wooden frame.
Then robin came bold to the kitchen door
Pecking at crumbs and looking for more.
The seasons have changed since I was a child,
Winter days are unseasonably mild
And I've just watched a polar bear die on the telly,
'Cause he hadn't the strength to fill his belly.
While his brother is hunting for life sustaining meat
The ice is melting from under his feet
And pale blossom unfurls on the tree in the sun,
Fooling us to believe that spring has begun.

Frankie Shepherd

The Gap

I was young - just skipping around -
Next thing I found myself on the ground
Consoled with an apple I tried a big bite
But oh mercy me, I had such a fright
Front teeth broken - beyond dentist drill . . .
How shall I sing now - with a trill?
I thought, as I gazed at yon cavity
What a powerful force - this gravity!

Beryl Mapperley

Power Of The Planet

It's February and I woke to a red sky
And sun like a ball of fire caught my eye
Cold and frosty, it's early in the year
Sun still shining bright, birdsong fills the air.

My bird table has four blue tits and what joy
Blackbirds too enjoying, fatballs and seed for all to enjoy
Violets in the garden, it's a sign of spring
Bluebells are showing clusters of green
Soon before you know it, the flowers will be seen.

Of course, there are weeds growing well
In every garden without fail they dwell
When weather gets warmer, there's plenty to do
Everyone will be busy, including me and you.

Then comes Easter, time to start planting
For summer gardens to be enchanting
Flowers, bushes, roses and vegetables too
Not just for us, but people passing to enjoy too.

After all the joys of pretty flowers
Autumn returns with leaves falling red
Then winter snow we dread
Because of icy roads and paths we tread.

Before you know it, Christmas is here
We look forward to the new year
And nature will provide beauty for all to see
Without fail for you and me.

Joan Read

Power Of The Planet

Power of the planet is vast with many things delightful
Shades of darkness, light and a sky so far away
Much scenery that is beautiful
The moon and stars to gaze at in the night always.

Power of the planet looks deep into the ocean
Plenty water to serve myriads of sea creatures
O'er all the globe brings in the spirit of cohesion
That love and peace may flourish with words from preachers.

Charge us with stewardship to follow guidance and sign
Not to pine but to crave
To work with power of the planet to preserve and to refine
Upon our hearts the power of the planet to engrave.

Pardon any disapproving thoughts or asking to prove
Give us for climate change an appreciating heart
Power of nature to be at rest or to move
Make us grateful for small or large mercies to have and to impart.

Power of the planet knows all about the Earth
Soil, water, growth and other nature's element
Making up the joy of mirth
All creatures give delight for this firmament.

So the power of the planet witnessing the seasons
Example in springtime growth and newborn first cry give cause
                                                    for praise
Our senses ponder over reasons
But sometimes woodrot and death takes us to the graves.

Olive May McIntosh-Stedman

Whirling Weather

Sing ding-a-ling embrace whirling weather
Lean forward to brace against the swirling storm
Cheeks flushed red from the heady graze of turbulent air
While eyes pinpoint spiralling leaves gusting on the wind.

Sing ding-a-ling embrace whirling weather
Cheer the taut flag flying high
Flapping and clapping in the windy blast
Sing ding-a-ling embrace whirling weather
Rounded jackets balloon in the squally clamour
As teeth are clenched in a grimacing mouth
Fists tightly enclosed in warming pockets
While scarves wildly flutter in agitation.

Sing ding-a-ling embrace whirling weather
Unkempt, windswept, rivers foaming at the mouth
Rough, unruly, mutinous breeze
Clashes and crashes against silhouettes tensely bent.

Sing ding-a-ling embrace whirling weather.

Pamela Sears

Summer Seascape

The sunlight wrinkles the sea
The way
Granny used to test the saucer of jam
To see if it was set,
We children watching her in the
Blackberry-fragrant, chilly scullery,
Sucking the juice from our still stained fingers.
    . . . And those long ago summers
Are as close as the foam now
Over my feet
The spray lapping
Lace patterns of coldness.

Karen Wood

When

When days are blessed with April showers
When gardens start to fill with flowers
When skies above are blue again
And sunshine always follows rain
Life's wonderful.

When cuckoos haunt the budding trees
When gardens hum with busy bees
When lazy days are dreamed about
It makes me want to stretch and shout,
'Life's wonderful!'

When all these things arrive at last -
When wintry days are in the past
When everyone begins to smile
It makes you stop and think awhile
Life's wonderful!

Hannah Yates

Spring Poem

The March lion is prowling on the hillside
Where sheep are sheltered safe from its wild way
By walls and between rocks, they huddle warmly
While nesting birds with song make sweet the day.

Flames licking the chimney, dragon with a thirst
Swift the tale of fire born, hot the ember
Which excites to flight the sparks that freely burst
Roaring from their cage as we remember.

March month has many weathers, moods and changes
In waterways, in land and under earth
But one thing is consistent and that thing is
The season of life's natural rebirth.

Kathleen Scatchard

Winter's Appeal

Frost forming patterns on grass and fences
A sharpening of the senses
Glowing faces, a red nose
Freezing fingers and tingling toes.

This is healthy, for you to enjoy
Shrieks of laughter from girl and boy
In odd little places snowdrops appear
Exquisite and beautiful, this time of the year.

The sky is heavy with snow on the way
Heralding a crisp cold February day
The snow falls, first it's light and not in a hurry
Then thicker in bursts and then a flurry.

A virgin-white perfect scene
Where no human being has been
Soon footprints in he snow
Cars slowly pass and the road begins to show.

Children love this weather
Old folk are at the end of their tether
But the beauty is all around
Bright days without much sound.

The beauty does not last for long
It is like the ending of a beautiful song
Will fade and disappear
Alas, it has gone for another year.

Olive Young

White Delight?

Snow, snow, snow
Fallen overnight, you know
So be careful how you go
For there too may be ice
Underfoot, not very nice,
For lack of care has its price.

Car drivers too must beware,
And take considerable care,
Making a mistake, do avoid,
For results could make you annoyed.

Looking at the garden all white,
It seems such a delight,
From inside, you don't feel cold,
But outside, one needs to be bold.

Some eighty years ago
One would have been out on the snow,
Making balls to throw
At sisters and brothers,
And maybe others.

Weather may be the same,
With old age, a different game,
But not to be deplored,
Just welcomed with due accord.

George Beckford

Summer

Summer fills the horizon
With shades of azure-blue
Swallows skim the treetops
As back once more they flew.
Golden sunlight filters through
Each tiny crack and space
Wild flowers cling and flourish
Like dainty, patterned lace.

The soaring lark ascends
High over fields and trees
Into a cloudless sky
Warbling above the breeze.
A haze of heat hangs low
Above the busy town
Where people long to move
To country, woodland, down.

Beneath a shady tree
With cooling drink, ice cream
Where there is perfect peace
And time to sit and dream.
These golden summer days
Leave earth so hard and dry
All creatures seek the shade,
On stone an egg would fry.

The temperature excels
The highest record set
Children just want to play
With water's cooling jet.
Oh lovely summertime
Bring cooling rain by night
Awaken dawn refreshed
As day springs into light.

Joan Heybourn

Islands Of Peace

These islands of peace
In a troubled sea
Provide a little rest
For me.

These tranquil isles
If I close my eyes
Will let me stay
Until sunrise.

These sandy shores
Are so discreet
And the sea caresses
My tired feet.

These islands of peace
That ease life's test
These tranquil isles
Are just the best.

Stephen P Sunter

Mother Nature's Quandary

The planet's getting warmer, things have gone askew
Mother Nature's in a quandary and doesn't know what to do.
Flowers out in the summer are still going strong
Like busy lizzies and geraniums - so something is wrong.

I noticed this morning four roses appear
It's now mid-November and they shouldn't be here
The violets are flowering as if it were spring
Strange things are happening - a global thing?

The glaciers are melting at both North and South Poles
Will they say there's a drought when this water flows?
The hole in the ozone layer is getting bigger
It's carbon dioxide emissions we figure.

Leave your cars at home, get out on your feet
Then the ozone layer may again be complete.

Enid F Thomas

In The Uluru Land

Under the outback sky
Far away from any city . . .
I was with perfect strangers
We saw the setting of the sun
Behind Ayers Rock
Dined under the stars -
A feast of barramundi
Kangaroo, emu, crocodile
And bush salads. We heard
The haunting sounds of a didgeridoo.

Desert night. How dark the night was . . .
The blackest black.

A candle was burning on each table
Strangers were conversing, dining -
We spotted a dingo watching us.
Very still, peaceful place.

This absence of sounds . . .
The tranquillity within.

In this darkness we stared at the stars
Something had happened with the sky . . .
Beautiful, amazing. We could see so much!
Someone shared with us all he knew
About the cosmos - dream time.

There we were . . . just us, in the red centre
And the universe. Reaching out
To the universe. In that place
Of not knowing. All asking
The same kinds of questions.

Claire-Lyse Sylvester

A Memory

They're funny aren't they
Those long-forgotten memories
That suddenly spring to mind
When you see something familiar?
Whilst walking through a playing field
At just the right time
At just the right light
On a warm summer's eve
There's a girl and a boy
Sitting on a bench
At just the same age as I was
In this long-lost memory of mine.
That's me sitting on that bench
With that girl
Many, many years ago
As a teenage inadequate.
That's me sitting next to her
On that bench overlooking the football pitch
Sitting together in the twilight
Too shy to speak
And too shy to move in for a kiss.
That's me there, who knows she is cold
Now that the sun has finally dropped below the trees
But is too afraid to put his arm around her
And just like many, many years ago
I know she is waiting for me to hold her
To kiss her
And to make her feel special.
But with every passing moment
The moment feels like it's gone
And as I walk past this young couple
Acting out my memories
I feel like I've aged terribly!

Matt Doran

Time Out

Cherry tree against the blue
Fragrant blooms of white green hue
Skyward reaching ladened arms
Whose buds unfurl their healing balm.

Western sun tints petals pure
Glints of golden amber to the viewer
As blackbird echoes its melody
Tranquil moments hold the key.

Take time out just sit and stare
Relax, inhale the mild spring air
Gaze beyond the bough of tree -
Imagine blue of sky becoming sea,
Its twinning branches reach Southern shores
Where exotic birds include macaws
Palms stand tall on silver beach
As yachts sail the coral reef
Whose shoals of neons iridescence gleams
As sunlight permeates the turquoise seas
There turtles dive through caves in deep
Then climbs those floral mountains steep
Within that crystal paradise gardens keep.

Now pondering the bough of tree
Reminiscing that distant scene
And how good it was to take time out.

Margaret E Richards

The Bluebell Wood

The misty haze of vibrant blue
Amidst the luscious green
In England's woods a brilliant hue
Most lovely to be seen.

Sunlight glinting through the trees
On bluebells thick and wild
A treasure for the world to see
A beauty undefiled.

The bluebell's beauty comes each year
To lift our spirits high
The delicate glowing mantle bears
An echo of the sky.

The bluebell wood's a special treat
The epitome of Spring
Swaying, dancing round your feet
Makes your glad heart sing.

The bluebell woods will always be
Most precious to behold
As the gentle flowers uncurl
The heavenly blue unfolds.

Walk in the woods on an early morn
With the dew all sparkling bright
On bluebells shining in the dawn
See Springtime's loveliest sight.

Mollie D Earl

Wonderful Summertime

To me, summertime is the best part of the year
The heat is wonderful and the aroma of blossoming flowers helps
my mind to clear.

For clarity is needed throughout the year and for me clarity always
comes with joy.
I truly believe that everyone having a joyful spirit, would create
a better world.
I guess some people will call me a joyful, spirited boy.

I tell you all that I am, what I am;
I'm someone who loves spicy food and who loves the
hot summer heat.
Something that goes great with the hot summer heat are the funky,
jazzy beats.

I love the feeling of waking up to the sunshine.
Sunshine comes from the sun which is a creation from the divine.

I love coming down in the morning to eat eggs and drink cold,
fresh, orange juice,
eating warm delicious eggs helps to fill me up and also warm up
my stomach
and drinking cold, fresh orange juice helps my mouth get loose.

As soon as I walk out the door, the breezy, cold wind touches my skin.
The breezy, cool wind helps to cool my skin and also helps me forget
about my sins.

Walking down the street through the heatwaves can only be
experienced during summer.
I've always found heatwaves interesting because you can
see heatwaves.
From a similar distance, similar to the waves created by a drummer.

The sight of the gleaming reddish-yellowish sun is always great to see.
This is a great sight for me because it reminds me of a lovely
buzzing bee.

Buying an ice-cold lollipop from the corner shop every day
is one of my favourite things to do during the summer and as I lick
the tasty lollipop,
I love the feeling of sensation, I don't know why, but the feeling
of sensation on my
tongue reminds me of water on a window going through the process
of condensation.

I really enjoy lying down on the warm, soft grass in my back garden
while baking in the sun.
I also like doing this while I munch on my spicy, meaty bun.
I find the whole notion of summer inspiring, spiritual and most
of all exciting.

Tawfeeq Elahi Samad

Ode To A Season Of Mists

The crackle of leaves underfoot
The mellow yellow of a birch branch
Here comes glorious autumn
With its seasonal scents of burned leaves
And most beautiful glowing hues
Nature offers stunning autumn colours
Gold, burnt-orange, purple, green
Every shade of colour in splendour
Autumn crocuses and chrysanthemums
In the ancient woodlands
Take in the vibrant reds and golds
Soak up the serenity of the cedar tree
Don't miss the glorious shade of blue asters
Sways with Japanese maples and acers
Bursts with red berries and mushrooms
Late October, when the clocks go back
There will be a nip in the air
And a soft fall of leaves in woods
So, I sincerely wish to you all
A crisp and colourful autumnal fall.

Victorine Lejeune Stubbs

Thank You

Let's raise our hands and thank our Lord
For the summer that's just gone by
Thank Him for the lovely flowers
And the sun up in the sky.

For the wonderful holidays we've had
In places far away
But most of all, let's thank Him for
His blessings given every day.

Now thank Him for the golden tints
On many shades of green
For combine harvesters and crops
And field mice rarely seen.

For spiders' webs, sparkling with dew
The last rose and the acorns
And thank Him that we're still here to see
All these lovely autumn dawns.

Lucy Williams

Tree Felling

And who are we as mere men
To bother nature now again
The ash, the oak, the sycamore
Who could ask for more
These beauteous trees
Yes, these we see in our land
So grand they grow to their maturity
But we in our brutality
Fell without feeling
And who are we in our stupidity
To bother nature now again?

Robert Walker

The Impeccable Gardener

When God made His lovely garden
The day was not quite gone,
He said I must create a gardener,
So He made the lovely Monty Don.

He gave him seeds
An assortment of trees,
Bulbs to plant in the ground,
And a mixture of flowers all around.

Now Monty was very inventive,
God said, 'Show me what you have made
What do you call these strange objects?'
Monty said, 'That's a hoe, a fork and a spade!'

He loves walking around his garden,
Whatever the weather, every single day.
He's plotting and planning his landscapes
Every step of the way.

Every now and again God says, 'Monty,
Are you pleased with the woods and the fields?'
He says, 'God I think I'm in Heaven
Every moment I'm at Berryfields.'

'Well if you're pleased I know I am,'
Said God, truly satisfied,
'The garden is yours forever,
My choice has been justified.'

So Monty has widened his horizons,
Not only does he garden in all seasons
He writes and broadcasts too,
He teaches lads to garden who have lost all reason.

And so he goes from strength to strength
Doing God's work as was planned,
We can all see what God had intended
When he took 'Monty' in hand.

Hazel Palmer

Ten Seconds Of Forever

In the tenth second of forever,
I looked my last upon this Earth,
At the bright blue sky
Soon to be gone in the blink of an eye.

In the ninth second of forever,
I saw the naked starving children
On the plains of Ethiopia,
And saw their tears dry on their faces.

In the eighth second of forever,
I gazed upon the world's people,
Of all cultures, race and creed
And heard their cries for absolution.

In the seventh second of forever,
I saw man's futile wars,
The murder of the innocents,
I saw men wet themselves in fear,
For today was our day to die.

In the sixth second of forever,
I gazed upon the widespread panic,
Of people fleeing for their lives
With no place to run or hide.

In the fifth second of forever,
I felt the hot breath of man,
Taking its deep last breath,
Heard the start of its death rattle cry.

In the fourth second of forever,
I saw the fires burn the Earth,
The ground heaving beneath the onslaught,
The blue flames of destruction dancing their waltz.

In the third second of forever,
I saw the angels of vengeance
Their white, red, brown and black horses on the wind,
And heard the swish of death's scythe.

In the second, second of forever,
I saw my beloved's face engraved in my soul,
Felt his lips kiss me for the final time,
Felt our souls join together for eternity.

In the last second of forever,
I heard the martyr's prayers on the breeze,
Put the capsule in my mouth,
Said my final, 'Amen.'

The world spoke no more . . .

Carol Bradford

Cottage Flowers And Carriages

Out of the bright sunshine and into the
Dapple shade - within the whitewashed chapel
Everywhere adorned with garden flowers
From every cottage garden - they sat on window sills
The altar and hung from the ends of every pew
Flickering candles again from every cottage danced
On the window sills that sparkled with sunlight
The congregation stands has - slowly takes down
The aisle her father leads Ruth to Jacob
They stand in silence and a lifetime look and smile
Then the pastor takes charge and the organist begins
The first hymn - the pastor asks who takes this woman
And their world changes forever and spins on one axle
The village hall awaits with real ale and the finest fayre
Rooms over the stable block and a new way of life
The big house carriage awaits for the happy couple
As the farm labourer takes his parlour maid for his wife
The promises have been sealed - the chapel bells ring out
Back out of the dapple shade bedecked in fragrant hue
Showered in rose petals and good wishes from the villagers
This summer's day - a wedding day - but a village affair.

David Charles

Why Does The Earth Groan?

Why does the Earth groan?
Why do her seas roar with rage?
She gathers her airs to sow destruction
She shakes her frame and mountains fall
Great gouts of fire she exhales
And magma, her life's blood, wells up
Her veil she rends, the sun's arrows freely pass
Her poles melt and crumble
Yet who will pay heed?

Her people are too many
And she would ease her burden
She brings forth infertility
But they have eaten greatly of the Tree of Knowledge
She sends drought and famine
But they are crafty, versed in many skills
She spreads pestilence
But they have learned of her healing bounty
When will they pay heed?

When air is toxic
And her creatures, slow to evolve, fall victim
When beasts and plants gasp, choke and wither
And Man's defences fail to turn the tide
As oceans rise, invade the cringing land
And even great Leviathan, deep though he dive
Cannot escape the arrows of the sun
With Earth sere and barren
Then may they pay heed!

George A Baker

Spring Fever

I cannot tell why my heart thrills when standing with the daffodils
I cannot tell why they enchant me so
Bobbing in the freshening breeze to and fro
As I wander through the wood they catch my eye beside the brook
Standing with the crocus, the bulrush, the primrose in a shady nook

I cannot tell why my heart sings espying the little lambs in Spring
I cannot tell why they please me so
Gambolling with their sisters and their brothers in the sunshine's glow
As I wander through the farmland they chew the cud and call
Woolly and white, sweet and new, close to mother completing the view

I cannot tell why my heart cries when trees burst into bud on high
I cannot tell why they touch my soul
Perfect and pure as the new leaves begin to show
As I cycle through the lane, life springs forth from their branches again
Sheltering the path from the wind and from the rain

I cannot tell why my heart dances when wood anemones push
                                         through the soil
I cannot tell why they charm me so
Amongst the ferns and grasses welcome and wee and winsome
As I wander across the common, their faces smile and shine
Creating a Springtime carpet of pink and green and white

I cannot tell why my heart laughs when watching catkins blossom
I cannot tell why they tease me so
Lightest green, brightest lemon against the barren copse
As I motor through the countryside they speak to me of Spring
Blowing and wafting on the witch-hazel, whilst robins
                               and blackbirds sing.

Margaret Bennett

The Stream

Gently flows the stream from the culvert,
dropping from the weir,
running bright and clear,
rippling over rocks along the way;
and the music that it makes has steady rhythm,
a pattern of its own
with variance of tone
as it journeys on its way toward the sea.

Mildly flows the river from the culvert,
pounding down the weir
with a force creating fear,
tumbling like a torrent on its way;
and the thunder of its sound is truly awesome
surging through the creek
with a resonance so bleak,
reflecting power and anger as it grows.

Energy is flowing in the stream out from the culvert,
passing o'er the weir
as it travels down by here
pouring past the shrubs on either side;
and the music that it makes creates a simple message -
that its moods ever changing
show Nature's always ranging
through the orchestra of life where'er it goes.

Gently flows the stream above the culvert
until the rains invade
and anger is displayed
as its strength increases, joined by other sources;
and the music that it makes may be heard by streets around -
a pattern of its own
from an origin unknown
within the hills and mountains all around.

Ann Voaden

Spring Returns

We get a large buzz from the season
Every morning brings a different reason
When life takes on a new perspective
Giving us more purpose, to be reflective.

It is a season which makes us light-hearted
Forgetting the gloom, which has just departed
In a gentle breeze, the corn will sway
Upon pleasant pastures we see stacks of hay.

There is a cornucopia, of much that will please
Birds sing in chorus, upon branches of trees
Brighter mornings and lighter nights
Bring a plethora of such fresh delights.

There are redolent scents and a myriad of hues
That spring has returned we find so many clues
It's a time when people's hearts seem to lift
This beautiful season is a wonderful gift.

Daisies and roses and tulips will grow
Silence is shattered with a cockerel's crow
Reinvigorated with what stares us in the eyes
Awakening each morning to a golden surprise.

Of insects then, we start to see traces
From the earth, the trees and other dark places
Early mists are dispersed with sudden showers
We are presented with a bounty of bewitching flowers.

Once naked bushes, now covered in green
A multitude of wasps and bees, can be seen
Daffodils and buttercups, add an extra touch
This is a season which we love so much.

Caterpillars metamorphose into butterflies
White clouds will float in the skies
Pampered with glorious delights
No other season can give us such sights.

Brian W Ballard

A World Too Far

In the wink of broken morning
Like the still of deathly night
Ideas for life are dawning
Like a spray of piercing light.

Waiting like the mountains
To see the braver skies
Futile like the fountains
Like tears behind your eyes.

The world is closing down tonight
Like boarding for a storm
A sun that sets the ground alight
And clouds that seem to mourn.

Pining like the rivers are
To flow back to the source
Have we gone a world too far
Will we show remorse?

Andrew Bott

Winter 2006/7

Why do you complain?
You wanted more rain
Now it's coming again
It bears you no ill
The reservoirs fill
But more's coming still
The rivers are flowing
And the lakes are growing
Where's it all going?
Will there still be a water shortage?

Catherine Blackett

The Honeybee

For nectar from selected crops
Collected in such minute drops
Then sold in jars in many shops
My thanks to the honeybee.

For dedication of each hive
To forage, search and to provide
One means to help us to survive
My thanks to the honeybee.

For perfection spread on crispy toast
Or ideal topping to flaked oats
The good it does to lungs and throat
My thanks to the honeybee.

For tasty treats it's given me
On fresh-baked scones I have for tea
My humble thanks will always be
To each hard-working honeybee.

Brian M Wood

Beauty Of Our Days

Daily routine, the sunset
And as it must follow, the night comes
Fallen so deep into the world beyond
Until there is a sound of songs
Birdsong, making melodies
From my dream into my bedroom
From upon the trees whence sound travels
Remind me a thing, of a fresh morning
For as sure as the morning comes
Is as sure our beauty comes.

Michael Odega

Winter

Winter slinks in like a brindled cur,
A coyote creeping through leafless trees.
Saliva stalactites drip from its fangs. Its fur
Grows dank and the icicles freeze.

Famished, it peers through narrow slits,
Through amber pupils that threaten pain.
Plump in the snow a cock-pheasant sits
Then clatters away from its cold domain.

Like an eel or a lamprey with sucking jaws,
Winter slithers across the ice.
In ermine, a hare on twinkling paws
Escapes hibernal sacrifice.

A ravenous pi-dog, winter longs
With lolling tongue and lustful breath
To interrupt the robin's song
And do the nightingale to death.

Red as a berry on the bough,
The twittering robin salutes the sky.
It contemplates extinction now,
Observing winter slink off to die.

The nightingale, perched on the eaves,
Echoes the redbreast's sweet finesse
Of holly berries. The whipped cur leaves
And snowdrops usurp the universe.

Norman Bissett

Stoke Bruerne On The Grand Union Canal

Stoke Bruerne in summer sunlight
Brought birds and boats together
Moorhen and mallard without fright
Were swimming on the water.

Another moorhen nesting there
Upon a branch that floated
Made such a noise for just to scare
A canal coot she'd spotted.

Along the bank and into fields
More fauna I soon spied
Cooing pigeons perched up high
And lazy sheep there laid.

The flora roundabout that grew -
Rose hips and blackberries blue
Stinging nettles and teasel wild
And trees of every hue.

Above the Blisworth Tunnel high
The taller trees there grew
Amongst them was the locust strong
Whose fruit the Baptist knew.

Returning to the boats one saw
Reminders of sweet nature
Blackbird, Mudlark and Tarka too
With Poppy for good measure.

David Oliver

What Have You Done To Our World?

What have you done to our world man?
What have you done to our world?
We are getting very annoyed
Because the 'ozone layer' is being destroyed
What have you done to our world?

With aerosol sprays and smoke pollution
Let's stop these things, it is the right solution
We are sweltering in the atrocious heat
And just too hot to get a bite to eat.

What have you done to our world man?
What have you done to our world?
Tempers are getting very frayed
And everyone is so dismayed
What have you done to our world?

Train lines are beginning to buckle
Causing a few to have a chuckle
It certainly isn't a joke
When you cough a splutter in exhaust smoke.

What have you done to our world man?
What have you done to our world?
Could this global warming possibly be a warning?
What have you done to our world?

Violetta Jean Ferguson

Penguins

While it's blowing an icy gale
Three penguins head for the DFS sale,
'Can we get some herring?'
'I'm not sure.'
'But I hope there'll be bargains galore!'

Wendy Elizabeth Day

Childhood Memories Of Spring

I'm sitting here and thinking
Of the lovely world God made;
The mystery and the majesty
Of His work will never fade.

My mind goes back to childhood
As I romped through meadows green
Or watched the white clouds scudding by
Or paddled in the stream.

I loved to watch the swifts in flight,
The industrial ants and bees,
The pearly-pink of tiny shells,
Polished by turbulent seas.

The majestic moon in a velvet sky
Festooned by a myriad starts,
Was a magical sight to a tiny child
Crouched behind nursery bars.

By day the sun caressed the world
Burnishing trees and flowers.
What a great delight to laugh in the rain
And spy a rainbow through the showers.

Light glancing across the white-tipped waves,
The glistening pools, the golden sands,
Gave way, at night, to the lighthouse lamps
Sweeping across the silver strands.

It's good to have such memories;
They bring me peace of mind
When I'm afraid to question God -
Because now I'm almost blind.

When I began to lose my sight
I railed against my fate,
But peaceful now I revel in memories
Of the beauty of God's estate.

Monica O'Sullivan

August

The grass is going brown.
Small dog is restless
first lying in sun, then shade
while towels hang motionless
on the line, bleaching.
A small black fly samples
red wine left in a glass.
The euphoric drowning
is over too soon.
A yellow helicopter passes low
its blades whizzing my thoughts
away like satellites.

Distraction comes easily
memories of summers past
slide behind the eye:
a miraculous, terrified crab
trapped in a plastic bucket,
collecting cockles from the estuary
'Look for the bubbles',
bike rides and soggy sandwich picnics
dancing in mud at a pop festival
feeding a beach fire with driftwood
and singing while the sun goes down,
smooth skin touched.

Now on a hot summer's day
I hang out washing,
the grass turns brown.

Maggie Andrews

The Seasons

Spring
Spring is the season that bursts out for us to meet
Bringing forth spring flowers for us to greet
Forming little tight buds on shrubs and trees
Awakening plant life for us just to please
Birds are mating and building their bests
Spring is the season awakening from rest.

Summer
Summertime, the countryside is lush and green
No prettier sight could there be seen
Fluffy white clouds now adorn the sky
Birds are flying way up on high
The big warm sun, rising in the east
Summer is the season, one cannot beat.

Autumn
Autumn is the season the colour for rest
Birds are departing and leaving their nest
Leaves on the trees turn golden and brown
With undue haste fall gently to the ground
This is the season, nature takes a good rest
Autumn is the season getting ready for the next.

Winter
Winter is the season we find frost on the ground
Gentle white snowflakes float steadily down
The trees now stand so stark and so bare
No one would think that there was still life there
Ice on the ponds makes skating a real treat
Winter is the season so cold and so bleak.

Leonard Butler

Summer

Take a look around you
What a beautiful sight you'll see
A world so full of colour
There's no better place to be

Summer flowers are in full bloom
And wildlife's all around
Birds are warbling up above
It is a lovely sound

The sun is shining brightly
Outside the children play
Their mirthfulness fills the air
Throughout the light of day

Families, they take time out
For a special get-together
Pack their bags and off they go
And make the most of summer weather

The picnics in the countryside
And trips down to the beach
Help us to relax awhile
Pushing life's worries out of reach

The summer is a time to chill
To take in those summer rays
To explore the beauty of our world
Before regressing to our normal days

The summer's not perpetual
So make the most of it
We all know it won't be long
Before the autumn months have hit.

Julie Preston

The Approach Of Spring

The frost-shimmering rooftops
Vied in brightness with the light
Of bright spring sun.
In the woods an orchestra tuned up
With whistles, chirrups and perfected phrase
Squirrels interspersed territorial chatter
The restless sea beyond hummed in chorus.
One lone daffodil stood proud
A bugle reveille to its peers
Defiant of the icy soft-brushing breeze
Still nostril tingling and toe curling.
Pulsing of the tree sap rising seemed
Palpable, as leaves and blossom fidgeted to escape,
Raising hope that life began again -
Those clinging, claggy days of winter discomfort
Soon to be banished, by days such as this.

Di Bagshawe

The Reason For The Rain

Coming from the supermarket in a shower of rain
I was feeling miserable and started to complain
But the shower soon slackened and the clouds began to part
Rays of sunshine breaking through, lightened up my heart
Then my eye was drawn to the embankment nearby
Where in a flash of black and white, a pied magpie flew by
Despite the busy car park noise, the bank was filled with song
From birds perched in the bushes, dotted all along
The bank was golden with the gorse and pretty soon, I knew
It would be clothed in clouds of pink, as willow-herb followed through
The mountains wrapped around the town in misty shades of green
Where often after stormy showers a rainbow can be seen
Reflected from a waterfall or a mountain pool
Nestled in the woodland, quiet, clear and cool
All at once I realised I'd been wrong to complain
As Nature's beauty showed to me, the reason for the rain.

Pamela Evans

Animals Give Their Love To Me

I love animals and they love me
They aren't prejudiced at what they see
They aren't bothered about my obesity
They aren't ashamed of me
They aren't judgmental
They aren't bothered who I am or what creed
What sex I am, colour or what breed
They come to me, I treat them respectfully
Whenever I am upset they sense it
They come to me with comfort guaranteed
They know when I am crying inside, lonely
They know when I am confused, happy or sad
They know when I am in need
They come to me with a loving hug
They know I will never hurt them
They have seen I treat them respectfully
They can see into my soul when they look
Into my eyes, they can feel my emotions
They want to wipe away my tears when I cry
They bring me joy, love and peace
My trust in them I can release
All God's creatures are full of God's light
When one of them dies, light turns into night.

Jenifer Ellen Austin

Canvas

The mixture of yellow sunshine
And blue precipitation
Creates the composition of virescent life
Flourishing secondarily from primary sources,
And the whole spectrum transpires across the Earth.
It is such a sight to behold
Through our ivory orbs
Illuminating our ebony canvas.

Anthony John Ward

Creation

Saturn rings the peeling of the dawn
Bellows pump the air throughout the morn
Solar rays disturb the dormant ions
Of matters, kept in waiting over eons
Moonlight bathes the barren, lifeless soil
Mother Earth sleeps, tired from tireless toil
Mercury moulds clouds of sylvan hues
Reflecting on the sea, a myriad blues
Lightning strikes and thunder rains its blows
Earth quakes and molten lava flows
Amoeba stir and break out of their shell
Squid squirt forth and sharks pell mell
Seaweed wades ashore and plants become
Floral tributes, basking in the sun
Bees buzz busily through the air
Pollinating colours with artistic flair
Pterodactyls soar in azure skies
Earth-bound apes gawp with envious eyes
A band of mutant monkeys, playing in the corn
Stone a songbird's treble to silence. Man is born!

Ian Tomlinson

A Sunny Afternoon

Quiet the place, once alight with noise
Now in the present
Neatly poised
Ready and waiting for all to see
Gently uplifting
A solace to me.

This reflection of loving
So gentle the scene
All the noise
A might have been
This gentle silence, a gift, a-shine
Given with love to this heart of mine.

Mary Hughes

The Four Seasons

Winter
The fragile blue planet
Lightning strikes the palatial Earth
With magnitude, hurricane winds prevail
Unimaginable twisters roaring like mad lions.

Blue, red, orange and yellow bursts
Electricity so powerful and intense
As the stormy sky turns black and grey
Where Man is vulnerable, weakened by Mother Nature.

Spring
With new birth across the beautiful landscape
Gorgeous bluebells and daffodils, God's hand at work
Beautifying Nature's miraculous art
Where spider webs hang in suspension.

Silver gossamer threads woven to perfection
Where madame plays a spiritual springtime duet
As the frost magically melts away
Where a million petals open in clear sunshine.

Summer
The great kingfisher darts upon a stream
Below water spiders, newts and tadpoles
Summertime so golden, fresh with wonder
Daydreaming lovers idling besides the park.

As the dapple of sunlight dances upon the water
Where swans and cygnets swim beautifully
And the heavenly sky paints a picture
Where a multitude of birds fly majestically.

Autumn
A million autumn leaves fall sedately
With a myriad of magical colours
Upon the wood a carpet of marigolds
Where gay children play so innocently.

As madame sits upon her garden swing
Thinking of love, chance and romance
Oh love me still my earthly man
And be mine for evermore, immortalised.

James Stephen Cameron

Springtime In Sefton Park

After the frost and snow of wintertime
A quiet falls over the Earth
Slowly the snows melt and everywhere it is felt
That the sunny days will be here once more

At the lakeside ducklings are running about
The little moorhens so cute and sweet
Nestling up to their mother, enjoying the good fresh air
Though independent upon their feet
They are so tiny the bread is crumbled for a treat
As they are fed by passers-by.

The fresh green of early spring
A lovely promise it doth bring -
A promise of light nights, warm sunshine
Outdoor games galore, picnics in the country
Holiday alongside the sea
In whichever country we decide to be.

Here, in Sefton Park, children fish at the lakeside
And vie with one another on a bicycle ride
Often there are concerts of every kind
Amongst the woods, flowers and mushrooms you will find
All in the springtime in Sefton Park.

Blanche Rice

When Nature's Mood Turns Black

The Rosebay Willowherb sways gently
In the summer breeze, the sun
Illuminates a web which the spider
Negotiates far better than any tightrope walker.
Birds majestically fly in formation
Like an immaculate aeroplane display
Yet this is far from an idyllic summer scene
For it's after the great flood and unloved lakes
Sparkle in the sun, swamping fields
A sight as transient as snow for

When Nature's mood turns black you cannot hide
Its fury sweeps our cosy world aside.

No, it's not an idyllic summer scene
A broken woman laments on her wall,
Ruined carpet and personal belongings
Are heaped in a sad and ugly pile,
The reeking, retreating water leaving
A cruel calling card in her front rooms
And now the reporters in their waders have left,
Checked out of their expensive, elevated hotels.
Global warming? An act of God?
It's all the same to this poor soul for

When Nature's mood turns black you cannot hide
Its fury sweeps our cosy world aside.

Guy Fletcher

The Butterfly

She slowly crawls upon the leaf
Delicate teeth nibbling, biting
Almost tenderly, yet hungrily
Savouring the sweet taste it brings.

Dainty feet cling to the stem
With caution, but also skill
And she carries herself to the stalk
Carefully pulling herself up, into hanging branches.

With the tedious work done
She settles down, curling up tightly
A tiny mouth opens slightly
And out flows a beautiful, silken layer.

As the silk wraps around her softly
Her still form is enveloped in warmth
Then she waits, closing shining eyes
Waiting, with serene patience.

The sun sets to twinkling stars
Their radiance bringing her tranquillity
With a graceful yawn, she unfurls herself
Creating a resounding crack on the hollow shell.

Through this opening emerges a soft velvet
Tinged with royal purple, and sky-blue
Following this velvet, she flitters out
Flying up past the stars to the moon.

Samantha King

The Eagle

Feathered sentinel, golden breast
Aching wings seeking rest
Below, a stream filling pool
Where salmon play in water cool
To spawn.
In a dying dusk
Ceasing to mate with a pink-tinged dawn.

The rested bird takes flight
Glides, hovers, turns
Towards the busy, bustling burn.
Shadows grow in a brightening sky
Fish doomed to die no longer play
In frenzied search seek a place to hide
As outstretched wings in silence glide.

Talons open, swiftly slide
Into silvered skin
Tapered filigreed fin
Blood spills when the hunter swoops
Here, the hunter kills.

With caution, red deer
Move to drink the water clear
No scent of strangers
Announcing dangers
In the pure, clean air
Swirling water of the pool
Sullied by blood of a battle cruel.

Who shows fear?
Bird or beast?
There are no guests at the eagle's feast.

Wings stretched, he soars
Upward, close to Heaven's doors
Battling with a wind that roars
To suck the dust from the valley floors
Below.

The hunter drops the lifeless form
Tearing pieces for his mate and newly born
She will wait
With hungry eyes
Beating breast
To take his place
In the eyrie
Let him rest
For he is weary
After his endeavours.

Below a Caillie calls
Incessant, freezing rain falls
From a Highland sky.
Forlorn cry
Of an eagle
Mixed with the scream of a hare
Its blood painting the bracken
No longer bare.

Ann Wardlaw

Clouds

In my world of chaos, I gaze at the sky
I admire the peace there is for a cloud way up high
I see faces of people I have known
Long-gone souls to the sky they have flown
I see a scowl and a smile for their view of a 100 mile

Over the mountains I watch them bubble
Blown from the sea, avoiding trouble
Bright white, grey, red and yellow
To watch and to see is wonderfully mellow

They don't notice me down here, my friends
They don't know how my soul makes amends
Untouchable, beautiful and free
Maybe one day, that's where I'll be
So, for now, I'll go on watching the clouds in my sky
The faces of friends floating by.

Steve Roberts

Ode To The Planet

The birds that sing above the trees
The fish that swim in clear blue sea
All the animals with different homes
All of nature to behold
Changing seasons that come and go
A force of nature to behold
As climate change becomes a goal
To save this planet that we call home
The future of our home depends
On whether we can make amends
To change the way we live our lives
In hopes they'll change before we die
To leave this planet to our children
In the hope they'll have a future
Let us hope this can be done
And then we know that we have won
To change this planet for the best
And hopefully forget the rest.

Amanda Beeby

Bleak Forest Trail

Twigs crackle underfoot,
low mist cloaks the steely brook,
a haunting moon hangs in the trees,
leaves scatter in the chilling breeze.
Feelings of great foreboding prevail,
sensing unseen creatures along the trail -
as if the forest were out of bounds
once summer's passed, along with the crowds.
Then, all at once, my heart is cheered
by the enchanting sight of a magnificent deer.
Now privileged to have walked this way
- though, in future, perhaps I'll come by day!

Debra Dando

What's Your Favourite Time?

Moon, moon, so yellow and bright
Light up darkness from black night
Sun, sun, shining so high
So golden and warm, high in blue sky.

Whoosh, whoosh, blows the wind so strong
Whistling, howling a strange song
Pitter-patter, down comes the rain
Making flowers happy again.

Brr, brr, wrap up warm from frosty chill
Don't want to catch a cold to make us ill
Shiver, shiver, white flakes of snow do fall
Building snowmen, big or small.

For every day brings something new
Always a favourite time for me and you
Come wind, rain, snow or sunshine
Seasons continue throughout time.

Mike Tracey

Spring

When mornings start with birdies song
And nature's breeding need is growing strong
Shoots start to show from dormant plants
'SAD' people will finally stop their rants
The days grow long and the nights get short
And lambs will dance and hares cavort
But we still may get occasional frost
When some new life sadly may be lost
Though this will be only for a short time
And the temperatures will begin to climb
When the big coats and hats have finally been flung
We can hopefully say that spring has now sprung.

Chris Leith

The Wind

Oh hateful wind
You have destroyed
In one foul deed
(And left a void)
Of forest green
And trees so fine
One storm-racked night
With vicious Hein.

Oh spiteful wind
I sigh when I see
God's wonderful gift
A lovely tree
Lying on the turf
Branches awry
Like arms stretched out
As in death's cry.

You cruel wind
Your destruction profound
It's painful to see
The desolation all around
No mercy was given
The power you displayed
Made dwarfs of great oaks
That had stood for decades.

Oh pitiless wind
I'll never forget
The suffering to Man
You did project
You tried his patience
Smashed all that matters
Deluged his habitat
Left him in tatters.

You tempestuous wind
The time will come
When nature and man
Will work as one
Make good the damage
Build once again
We'll always remember
That night of disdain.

William Stannard

Your Garden

There's no place like your garden
For, travel near or far
It's lovingly created
By your own hands which are
Guided to buy lovely flowers
Set out in colours bold
The end result is lovely
As each new bud unfolds.

The song of handsome blackbird
Comes floating through the air
He sounds to be a happy chap
Who doesn't have a care!
So, when you're in your garden,
Look around and see
The beauty that is there for you
In plant and shrub and tree
God's blessings are so bountiful
His work is perfect, too
As summer shows its glory
To lucky me and you!

Jasmine Grace Geddes

Wasted

The way of the world is coming to an end
Better to just shut up and swallow
Sit down beside me my immortal friend
And I'll tell you a story that's hollow.

Once upon a time, there was a unified land
So uncorrupt, unsoiled and white
Still untouched by the human hand
And where there was darkness, was light.

The sun was shining rays of love
And the storm was warm with pure rain
Our Lord was smiling from up above
And Judas and Jesus are friends again.

Angels flew past as cherubs played
Unicorns were running free
God was happy with the life He'd made
Not knowing that it would turn out to be . . .

Wasted beyond all recognition
Life has been torn to shreds
Nostradamus has come to fruition
Sending us all to our early beds.

The demons that have roamed this Earth
From the dawn, have begun to destroy
Casting their spells and singing their curse
Still abusing this world like a toy.

Lucifer's laugh is polluting a nation
This life has been turned inside out
The human treaty is in violation
Drowning in a sea of screams and shouts.

The many battles that we thought we fought
The wrong decisions have been made
We haven't passed 'Go'; we came up short
And next to God we are laid.

Jamie Barnes

The Garth That Is Martina's

Upon a road that I know more than never,
Travelled between two familiar spires,
Thereto a dwelling with shutters green,
With walls of lime and a plot of treasures;
The eyes that so lovingly surveyed,
A plan hatched for the intended look,
Therein beds lay strewn, as if no order,
No garden path this, none never she took.

Almost nature alone the force to model,
Pollination as each species claims its patch,
And harmony as not seen in any other,
On limited space, fresh soil to eagerly catch;
In a perfumery laid wild in which the air to fill,
The aromatic fragrance of lavender and rose,
In refraction each glance reveals a subtle change,
Colours of contrast and akin carefully chose.

In a planted sense 'tis a peculiar thing
A Cottage Garden whose appearance is wild,
As if seeds and bulbs were randomly strewn,
The natural look, more the dabbling of child;
But in this place, beauty is captured in many forms,
In sight and smell, intoxicated from shortened stroll,
With eyes closed, easier the gardeners heard,
Their unrelenting buzzing, with the wind, they toil.

In stepping out the door and for years depart,
Leaving your charges to their very own devices,
They'll not disappoint on your return to view,
No better you'd have done than all their choices;
It's inherent that order can go against the grain,
Nature has a course with the slightest of nudge,
And no better example than this garden I see,
More than a brief assist it'd gratefully begrudge.

Oliver W Barrett

Malvern

Malvern and its range of hills
Gave me in a few days of my life something
To remember.
Elgar's music fashioned there
I play all day sometimes so fresh, sometimes
Just an ember,
The evergreen fields, the winding roads,
The cottages nestling, make me glad to be
A member
Of this peopled world at present occupied
By some who can appreciate these views whether in July
Or December.
It would be sad to see these taken from us,
Ironed out and flattened by this modern age by those who
Just dismember.
But always will I remember Malvern.

Joan Elizabeth Blissett

Heralds Of Spring

Oh, how I long for spring
Time of growth for everything
After the snowdrops
So early and brave
Up come the daffodils
With a bright cheery wave
Dancing on green stalks
They fill us with pleasure
Nodding in breezes
Nature's own treasure
Heralds, which tell us of
Warm days to come
Saying be happy
For winter is done.

Patricia Susan Dixon MacArthur

Evening In Mijas

The twilight draped about us
like a Spanish dancer's shawl
its fringes stroking fingers
of the Costas jewelled shore

The main square's coloured lighting
twinkled, flick'ring in the breeze
as evening strollers gathered
round the Plaza's spotlit trees

The dusky little donkeys
trotted downhill to their rest
as music from the grandstand
strummed Paseo time is best.

Aromas spiced and salty
wafted out from every door
as cheery chefs enticed us
to their Tapas tasting lore

With steaming hot paellas
the fruity wines they poured
we sang and clapped and feasted
while flamencos tapped the floor.

Rosemary Keith

Summer Is Cumin In

Broccoli or chestnut? Cream of celery?
Carrot, coriander? Chicken stock or Brie?

Cauliflower, green pesto? Courgette, Emmantal?
Parsnip, yellow pepper? Cumin or lentil?

Savoy cabbage, bacon? (That could do a week!)
Tomato and spring onion? Turnip boiled with leek?

Oh, this summer cooking! Read what's on the tin
Toss it in your basket, put your apron in the bin!

Sheena Blackhall

Night

Cool on the cheek are the first airs of evening,
Fingers of darkness creep over the lawn
Feeling their way as the dusk, ever deepening
Senses the truth of the daylight withdrawn
Piercing the silence, the notes of the blackbirds
Bathe the whole garden in mystic delight;
Twilight, ephemeral, slowly slides backwards
Leaving the world in the arms of the night.
Nectar, its magical perfume distilling,
Soothes and excites every nerve in the nose:
Now the nocturne of the nightingale, thrilling
Remnants of day as it draws to its close.
Rising, the moon shafts her fingers of light,
Stealthily stealing the dark from the night.

Vaughan Stone

Disillusion

They lay back in the bed watching the moths
Fly round the light with the cracked shade
They found so amusing the first time they stayed.
And skirting the ceiling, the border of fat
Bellied cherubs entwined with lovers' knots.

His gaze wandered to the faded pink curtains
Hanging like rags from a dusty pole
She considered the old thatched cottage
With full blown roses trailing over the fence
And the girl sitting on a garland swing
As bluebirds danced around her head.

With a sigh they looked at each other
Then decided to call it a day
Their affair had lost its excitement
In an out-of-town shabby hotel.

Rosaleen Clarke

Summer

Summer, is the season I wish would stay
Beautiful chirping from the birds
That sensational scent of the bloomed flowers
That elegant blue from the sky.

Happiness surrounds me when summer comes
Smiling faces from children running in the park
Twinkling eyes from couples holding hands -
Summer, is the season I wish would stay
Where the sun shines forever.

But . . .
Some days are rainy in England
In summer - yes, unusual, but yet
Yet I still love summer here
As, after rain and sunshine comes

A glorious rainbow - such elegance
England summer is where I am and wish to be
And happy to be.

Afsana Taib

Prelude

Though gardens never diet,
they show what comes of exercise,
Queen Elizabeth rose run riot,
cut to size.

Hollyhocks with over reaching aims,
belly-dancing, touching toes,
age too soon to play their games,
end in hoary arthritic rows.

Honeysuckle's last minute sprint
labouring, losing leaves like weight,
briefly strikes a short-lived glint,
wilts away and falls too late.

Rosemary Benzing

The Oasis

It's daybreak at the oasis and in a hazy, yellow sky
The sun is rising with a vengeance and the temperature's already high.
Three restless nomads, robed and veiled, discard their blankets and
brew weak tea
And exchange anecdotes as they sip it, in the shade of an acacia tree.
Then tend their camels and round up the goats,
Which had been left to seek what they could find
In the inhospitable wilderness, where the sandstorms can send
a man blind.

It's midday at the oasis and by now it's forty degrees;
The date palms and reeds are gently swaying in the minimum
of breeze;
And the itinerant desert dwellers continue with their affairs,
Spreading their plaited mats in readiness for midday prayers.
Crickets chirp shrilly, breaking the silence with dull, repetitive tunes,
And the inescapable sun beats down upon the ripples in the dunes.

It's nightfall at the oasis and there's a sudden chill in the air;
The temperature plummets sharply, as the sun goes down in a flare.
The stark, dramatic landscape takes on a different hue,
And the burning sand no longer burns, and the sky has turned
dark blue.
The cameleers wrap themselves in goatskin coats and await
the coming of the morn
As a full moon casts reflections on the oasis until the sun at dawn.

Heather Pickering

Rainforest Land

The cattle may graze where once was jungle maze
Where panthers and monkeys did roam
We will see them no more on new pastures galore
Have beef cattle and gauchos their home

Oh rainforest land, you have lost to the progress of Man
Your wildlife and plants may give you some cents
But grasslands bring cash in your hand

The trees have been burned, Nature's way overturned
Precious topsoil eroded away, some discouraging word
Can often be heard 'cause black smoke covers sky all the day

Oh new desert land global warming may soon be at hand
We better take heed, exploitation and green
Soon may cause the extinction of Man

The climate will change, way back home on the range
Many floods will cause problems galore
The once fertile land, will be barren sand
Heavy rainstorms will fall more and more

Oh rainforest land son all your birthrights are virtually gone
Since you moved to the town, do you often feel down
When you see that your forests are gone?

There still might be hope, if we manage to cope
And replenish those vanishing trees
If our forests may live, we can pray God will give
All Mankind on His Earth a new lease

Oh rainforest land, your herbs might give new cures to Man
Before it's too late, we must reinstate
All that bounty we had from God's hand.

Ivar Kalleberg

A White Seagull

I wish I was
A white seagull
Bobbing on the
Blue, calm sea
Of the Santa
Ponsa, Mallorcan
Bay, happily
As a speedboat
Goes by, gently
Weaving, molten
Sun through my
Calming wings
Upon azure
Waves, golden
Blinking, winking
A white seagull
I wish I was.

Edmund Saint George Mooney

Summer Twilight

Light fades
Petals close.
Shapes changing with day's withdrawal.
Air is still,
Carrying sound un-bent
By the breeze's manipulation.

Just watered earth
Releases aromas
Rich and thick as the sweetest honey.
A settling occurs.
Subtle comfort movements
As the garden prepares to sleep.

Miki Byrne

Summer Squall

Charcoal clouds boiling over
The tempest ruptures
A heated argument of nature
Sheets of mercury tears stun me
Into momentary blindness
White lightning strikes
Spears of livid passion
And the fervent roar of anguish
Cleave the textile of sky
Leaves propelled feverishly
By wind's brawny throw
In desperate upheaval, tantrum
Then over in a heartbeat
Composed, amicable harmony
Absolution in a teardrop.

Elissa Michele Zacher

Summer Rain

The wonder of raindrops
Caught on a leaf,
On a blade of grass -
A snail's paradise,
On every single flower.

The colours of nature,
Shimmering red berries
Exquisite, awesome
Rain so soft . . .
So beautiful.

Cathy Mearman

Seaford Sussex

Early morning light across the bay
The mask of night has slipped away
Sun still to rise above the Downs
Awakening gulls venting raucous sounds

Sea sweeps pebbles up beach incline
Rattling rhythmically back into the brine
Pebbles rounded smooth by endless tide
Some if looked closely, fossils hide

Seashells, whelk cases, mermaids' purses
This strong spring tide, its wares disperses
Seaweed, bladderwrack, odours of marine
These natural objects set the scene

Sentinel cormorant stands on exposed rock
Outspread wings drying, taking stock
Mackerel shoal just offshore
Silver shimmering, splashing, gulls galore

Whitebait providing this frenzied feast
Sun now climbing Downs to the east
Sky pinked with red and gold array
The start of a beautiful summer's day.

Len Peach

Nights On The Shore

Oh midsummer nights of gentle breeze
Warmly wafting to inviting seas
Set in the redness of the burning sky
Where a dark blue mix of yellows apply
Calm is the resting glazed tide
Stars shine like tinsel set in a lighter blue
Shooting stars streaking through
I look into the distance of a twilight shore
Towns in glowing lights I saw
So warm is the comforting summer air
In a captured view, that can't compare
Romance springs to mind along the beach
Holding the hand of the loved one, you reach
And you kiss to the ocean's gentle touch

And with the striking view, moves you much
The shushing of the rhythmic tide
Smoothes emotions inside
How taken as together both in embrace
As the moonlight caresses softly in that place
And a memory that can't be forgot
In the instance of that sandy plot
Serenity paints an oil picture view
Of an ever kept moment with me and you.

Terry Powell

Polstead Pond

The rain started to fall hard, hopefully it won't last
Travelling through Hintlesham and Hadleigh, places from the past
When arriving at Polstead Pond, the downpour was fast
No fisherman out to throw a firm cast.

Relaxing for a while to have our lunch
Rings appeared on the water as the rain fell in a bunch
The sun shone through, everyone was pleased as punch
As I thought, the weather would improve, I just had this hunch.

How the weather can change within minutes, amazed us all
Suddenly, the reflections glistened through trees with droplets to fall
Gentle ripples followed as the fish approached the water's edge, giving
their call
And walkers headed off for an afternoon stroll, standing tall.

Standing by, with loaves of bread to break
Patiently we watched, no noise we must make
The carp lifted its head, slopping as it ate, followed by more on the take
Whilst the crumbs floated by the lonely old drake.

Adrian Bullard

The Water Lilies

A feast for the lovers of nature
Came into view as I strolled along the canal bank
For a carefully created space in the reeds
Exposes the lily patch and I wonder who I should thank?

Just who took the trouble to cut down those reeds?
Like me, did this stunning view he want to share
The pink and white flowers opening up with the sun
Which would otherwise have been hidden there?

Someone else has a love for nature like me
It is such a shame more people don't care
For the countryside's alive with such sights, sounds and smells
And they are there for us all to enjoy and to share.

Don Woods

Thunderstorm

Light is dimming in the forest,
Humidity hangs in the air,
Wind changing direction, gathers force,
Black thunderclouds scud across the sky,
Leaves are spiralled upwards back into the trees,
Suddenly there's quiet,
The forest is holding its breath,
Birds have stopped singing, everything is still!
The storm breaks, thunder rolls,
Bolts of lightning strike the ground,
The heavens open,
Drenching everything in rain!
Where do they go, the creatures of the forest?
Birds shelter their young in the swaying branches,
The storm is over as quickly as it began,
Raindrops are glistening on blades of grass,
Birdsong fills the air and sun-kissed eyes awaken
Nature's never-ending cycle
- begins again!

Margaret Pedley

Brrrr

Winter is approaching fast
The chill is in the air
Some days feel warm
And some feel colder
Whatever should we wear?
And when it finally hits us
We dread the freezing cold
And long for summer sunshine
And days that gleam like gold
But whatever the weather
We must all persevere
And tolerate what Nature sends
However severe.

Edward Hill

Summer

Summer will be warm this year
Your hand in mind beside the stream
The sky will imitate your eyes
And sun will blaze with jealous zeal.

Though love came late to you and I
It ripened long, its fruit the sweeter
Tissue wrapped, our fragile thoughts
Are crystal clear and priceless rare.

We shall sit beneath the oak
In careful shade as noon departs
Your tilted hat bring straw-touched dreams
And I shall meditate on joy.

The evenings shall delight in stars
And soft the moon will call our names
Clasped, our hands will join our hearts
Eternal love shall be our vow.

Pam Davies

Summertime

I like jumping around
And sing a song

Go to my grandma
For a cuppa

Play out outside
On the lawn

Eat ice cream
And watching repeats

Summer nearly over
Can't wait for another.

Bav

Summer Sun

As the warm summer sun sets serenely, where the sky meets the sea
It seems at peace with the world, as it fades from sight gracefully

And a cool salty breeze, drifts across the golden sands
As we stroll along the shore together, holding one another's hands

A calm, quite, stillness surrounds us
As night gently replaces day

Relaxed, feelings of contentment overwhelm us
And slowly we daydream away

Is this Heaven on Earth, we ask?
Holding our breath, as if to make time stand still

Taking a moment, to remember
For feelings like this cannot be conjured up at will

But then as the warm summer sun sets serenely, for both you and me
For others it simultaneously rises like a phoenix from the sea

Bringing joy to those it touches, lighting up their day
As the warm summer sun continues along its merry way.

Paul Taylor

Season Called Spring

Oh, how I love the season called spring
And all Mother Nature's creations it does bring
Like butterflies and bees and birds on the wing
And the arrival of the daffodil such a beautiful thing.

Yes, spring to me is a glorious time of the year
Especially after the winter, so cold and drear
A time to see nature's handiwork at its best
And all the lovely colours in which the countryside is dressed.

To see the pink and white blossom that adorns the trees
Swaying to and fro in the warm spring breeze
And the new growth on the hedgerow where birds nest and sing
Oh, how I thank Mother Nature for the coming of spring.

Anthony V Carlin

A New Leaf

The beginning

Frosted white crystals, turn to liquid
And saturate the earth
A rainbow of hues immersed in green slowly returns

In her home of freshly nipped grass
Discarded roots, and rotting vegetation
A proud Mama keeps vigil over her future

Only yesterday
A tall, naked, stem stood unnoticed
Today a solitary flower
Battles the wind
Its scent attracting a swarm of bumblebees

One lone leaf leads the way
The first to arrive
Now the maple tree has a name

Mother Nature is standing
Yawning
Stretching
At last she is awake.

Johana West

Special Moments

A shaft of light
Shone through the clouds
Just a beam, but brilliant
So welcome in its flight.

I held out my hand
Wanting to touch it
But it slipped through my fingers
Like grains of sand.

Its beauty
Radiating through the sky
Spreading, then disappearing
Sending its beam, from way on high.

Then the birds appeared
Like phantoms in the light
Floating through beams of radiance
Then swooping in their flight.

As the clouds closed
The beauty was gone
But I had the memory
Which lingers on.

Joan May Wills

Summer's Arrived

Blossoms bursting out into the tree
To making it look like summer's arrived
Birds singing sweetly to tell you
Summer's arrived
Squirrels climbing up and down trees
To tell each other, summer's arrived
Bunnies bouncing up in the air,
Making the letters, summer's arrived
Children merrily playing on the beach
Chattering and tittering
Telling each other that summer's arrived
Everyone shouting and singing,
Summer's arrived!

Anna Paul (9)

Seasonal Miracles

Spring is the time for renewal and growth,
When the past season's pallor is pushed aside.
Days become longer and smiles seem brighter,
And the flowers in gardens beam with pride.

Animals emerge from their long hibernation,
Frogs return to their place of birth,
Blossoms bring colour to dreary old streets,
And birds sing sweetly for all they're worth.

We bask in the glory of these warmer days,
Admiring everything there is to see;
But of all the miracles we could perceive,
The migration of birds is the greatest for me.

Annabelle Tipper

Spring's Beginnings

It's a beautiful day
Nothing's getting in my way
Bees they are a-buzzing
Sun's bright, as I watch the children play
Birds are singing, spring's here, people say
The sky is painted blue
Frosts have all gone
Frogs are croaking
In my paddling pool my feet will get soaking
All good things happen in May
For with my lovely husband and child I'll stay
For spring is the most lovely time of the year
Flowers smell wonderful for all to see
It's springtime now for you and for me.

Rosalind Ann Webb

Summer

Flowers lift their faces to the sun
A new day has just begun
Fields and meadows of verdant green
Summer rain, fresh and clean
Running streams crystal clear
A sweet sound to the ear
The timid fawn from the bracken peeps
Around the bushes a sly fox creeps
Woodland trees gently sway
High above swoops a bird of prey
Butterflies flutter in erratic flight
The day's warmth drifts into the coolness of night.

Jenny Parker

Stop Blubbering, It's Only A Whale

If you hear my cry from the ocean deep
Will it stir your soul, does it make you weep?
It's a sound I use as my calling card
Your eyes will mist if you listen hard

To lose my song is to lose all hope
For a better world, how can the system cope?
Take away my reflection, your narcissistic man
Remove my name from your cat food can

Break up your harpoon and exploding shell
That inside me pain, delivered from Hell
No more my ambergris to float on summer's warm seas
That hides your smell from others to please

Just welcomed you into our waters as kin
Your sonic noise, pollutants and high frequency din
We never get angry, just evolved to survive
But with God's help let us take you on one last, deep dive.

Charles Keeble

Marigold's Cottage

She lives in a cottage on the edge of time
Her garden an ocean of yellow and green.

Nimbus clouds dance their way across
The indigo sky.

A tabby kitten frolics in the shadows
Chasing an imaginary friend.

Marigold picks wild blackberries and mushrooms
That grow in the woodland aplenty.

Makes jam and vegetable pies - sits them on
The window sill to cool in the breeze of the evening.

Vicky Stevens

The Waterway Of Life

The Mississippi, the waterway of life
With its many moods and seasons, as it is with life
Rich and full of promise and intrigues of the night
Your deepest waters, calm and smooth, the danger out of sight

The blackest whirlpool of deep sorrow
And the brilliance and the best of all tomorrows
The dark wooden avenues that block out all the light
And then the glittering avalanche of cascading might

The sudden deathly still, when fog shrouds out the light
And images like sceptres pass, unnoticed out of sight
Your lonely and uncertain courses
Travelling alone but with great resources

Your strength is there, we feel your might
See the pulsating heartbeat of your tonight
The wayward pull of your current so strong
You captivate all who journey along.

Doris Hoole

Summer

Summer's in June, I feel I need to bloom
The first kiss from a rose, smells of lips from the heart
Whereby I don't want it to fall apart, but to get lost in my soul.

I'd rather sip cool beer and remember it here
If only the ocean was as close to me like the breeze
And the sky, of times gone by.

I'd remember days from sunshine cakes, to chewing hay
Sweltering girls and men, drooling for the summer rain
From the young to the old, that summers have shown
That I'll never forget my first kiss from the rose.

S B Ally

Words

You edit these words
Fine as they are implicit
Coveted by winter coats and shade
As if snow was a memory of summer
And light was a lie

Across the sand we smell oil
Pulsing like an eagle's heart
Racing up high to dive down
And spear prey

All around us words
Furnishing our rooms, our dreams
Our votes caught within our wallets
Snagged like crazed marlins
Struggling against death

Desert spectres fill our streets
Blinking eyes to shield the sand
Tripping on the tiptoes of the future
We wait as if caught in a stammer
For truth

Carve the meat, the words
As you might a bug
Let it bleed on holy ground
Watch the meaning, fill cracks
And gaps
And witness their truth

The words hide in your pocket
Lying snug against your thigh
We surrender them to autumn rain
Awake, against a September sky.

Mack

Summer Rain

In that raindrop
Of glimmering suspension
On a leaf tip after summer rain

In the step of that man
Avoiding cracks on concrete
Mindless obstacles to manoeuvre

In the vibrancy of that colour
Red, orange, perhaps lime-green
Tropical take against chocolate skin

In that melodic phrase
An unusual sound or
The voice that utters and sings

In those silent tears
That hunched back protecting
A heart breaking soundlessly

In that roar of thunder
The flash of lightning
Rumbling and crackling to Earth

In a child's surprise
That delighted laughter
An innocent, spontaneous smile

In those abandoned shoes
Placed just so, waiting
The return of feet to fill

You're everywhere
Always there
Waiting to inspire.

Jacqueline Smith

Snowflake

With magnificent grace
The jewel in the skyline
Brown eyes fixed on mine
Strode toward me
My heart raced
As the tower
Of ivory and amber
Closed the space
Between us
Her vibrant colours
In sharp contrast
With nimbus clouds
Then distracted
Tilting heads skywards
Animal and human
Watched snowflakes fall
Her tiny mouth open
In a magical moment
I saw the giraffe, taste snow.

Jennifer James

The Rain

The rain
It's here again
Angry drops of water fall
Thrashing down
One and all
As we all nearly drown
Pools and floods
Splashing, splotting
We're all very wet
It hasn't stopped
It hasn't yet
Too much water
Too much rain
The weather has gone quite insane!

Theresa Hartley-Mace

Spring 2008 Is . . .

The beginnings and promises
Of nature's things
The musical pieces
Most every bird sings.

Last year's caterpillars . . .
Forgetting their crawling
Leaf-eating phase, experiencing thriller
Solo flights; soaring, then sprawling.

The boast of avenues and parks . . .
Horse chestnuts huge
Candles beckoning remarks
Before the deluge.

Of those petals to ground
Then begins schoolboys' wait
For such *months* for those round
Natural toys they all fete.

Gillian Fisher

Lost In Space

L ost
O
S
T

I n
N

S pace . . .
P irouette
A cross the universe
C ircling the
E arth . . . endlessly.

Kath Cooley

Owl

Grey on the dusk of night,
Hooded against a sky
Dusk as yourself, and bearing out
Awe to tranquillity . . .

I saw you cower and stay,
Then rise, hover and quiver,
Round-cowled shape on the cloudy play,
Glance in the dim, and shiver.
Shake down-plumage and wing,
Silent, a great moth, out
Into more than evening,
Sabbat-bound, half-devout
Masque in the solemn rout,
Half-menacing . . .

Veiled for an instant on the chimney stack,
Then off and fly . . .
Lost in the shadow-wrack . . .

Elsa Ivor

Autumn Love

Autumn sing a song to me
The air I feel
Blossomed with love
Autumn kindness is so great
For autumn prolonged her leftover rays
For though winter
Is about to call
Her farewell she stalls
Autumn bid a note so sincere
God be with you
Until next year.

Carolie Cole Pemberton

Summer Days

Boys and girls with happy faces
Parents loaded down with cases
Ice cream, pancakes, doughnuts too
Waffles, cokes and barbecue
Sea and sand and candyfloss
Crabs in pools of rocky moss
Donkeys up and down the sand
People sunning getting tanned
Water sports and yachts afloat
Skiers follow speeding boat
Deckchairs out and bands they play
Gardens with their grand array
Boats on lakes and kites in flight
Water craft tie up for night
Evening shows with well-known stars
Fish and chips and crowded cars
Fair and roundabout in motion
The stillness of a peaceful ocean.

Catherine Armstrong

Winter

Winter is the coldest season, going for a walk in winter
To catch a glimpse of rippling stream
Seeing a little winding path, gnarled oak stripped of their leaves
Seemingly lifeless trees, stately fir trees to see
Dull, cloudy day, a bitterly cold day
Desolate and deserted
I see footprints in the snowflakes
That lay on the ground and observe
There are people around
Nice to be home again
Where it's cosy and warm.

Anita Shedlow

Where Have All The Flowers Gone?

I am a child here in 2087
Looking back through history
To a world once full of colour
And our grandparents fancy-free.

Yes, just 80 years ago
They spoke of global warming
And said the climate was about to change
But they didn't heed the warning.

'Think green, take care and do your bit.'
The words rang loud and clear
But their apathy, greed and laziness
Has cost this planet dear.

Trees and flowers are now but dreams
By thoughtless man destroyed
Our world, now grey and bleak and sad
Our life no longer enjoyed.

We children are now like zombies
Devoid of fun and play
Shut in our techno pods (called home)
Never seeing the light of day.

Judy Rochester

Seasons Of Plenty

Corn is ripe
Apples, pears of plenty
Raspberries or blackberry pie
Hedgerows of covered honeysuckle scent
Swaying trees, gather thoughts
Singing song, birds roost for the night.

Alan Hattersley

The Baby Blue Tit

A little baby blue tit
Came to visit us
Very short of feathers
More a ball of fluff

Calling to his mother
In a baby blue tit talk
Hovering round the garden path
In a bouncy blue tit walk

I knelt just down beside her
And she hopped upon my knee
She stood awhile in stillness
Then she flew into a tree

A little fledgling blue tit
As pretty as can be
I'd never met a blue tit
Oh how she honoured me.

Ray Ryan

Spring

Oh, the mystical energies of spring,
Such wondrous joys it does bring,
There are buds and flowers, birds that sing,
Sunshine and showers waken everything,
This bright new world, we call spring.

May you all share this wonderful feeling,
Bringing upliftment, happiness and healing,
Tall golden daffs, shine their glory everywhere,
For all God's living creatures to share,
Oh, the mystical energies of spring!

Stella Bush-Payne

Into Autumn

Early this morning as I walked
Through meadows sweet
Butterflies were dancing
There about my feet.
Walking on into the cornfields
Where half the fields now ploughed
The sky above was azure-blue
Laced with bits of fluffy cloud.
The sun rose over the treetops
Casting its golden glow
Across the ripened barley
Still standing in a row.
Waiting for the combine
To gather in its grain
This will be the last to cut
With luck before the rain.
Where the plough's been busy
In the field next door
The crows are scratching
Over grain left upon the floor.
As I walk on into the woodland
The first rustle of an autumn breeze
Cooling after the heat of summer
Down come the first of the leaves.
The squirrels are chasing up and down
Teasing the dogs at play
While the woodpeckers are
Tapping in a melancholy way.
Back to the meadows we briskly walk
After a dip in the stream
To walk again with the butterflies
Sit for a while on a seat and dream.
Watching the gathering rain clouds
Now darker, threatening rain
Time to go home and face the day
Before we come back again.

Irene Keeling

Urban Delight

It is 7 o'clock; you've just opened your eyes
The east rising Sun streams in your room, where you still lie
The morning chorus of sparrow and blackbird
A song you never tire of, even though it's one you've already heard
You lay a while as the serenade goes on
Just for a while you are the only person alive
And only you can hear this beautiful song.

Alas, you must rise and leave this bliss
But not to worry, that's not all there is
In your kitchen, you make your tea and toast
Out of your window you catch sight of the thing you love the most
It is Spring and things are starting to rise to the Sun
It is the time of year where new life has begun.

Daffodils nod their knowing heads in the breeze
Leaves are budding on waking trees
Your early morning hosts are finding food and working hard
You have to smile, all this going on in your small backyard
You get dressed with a spring in your step and a permanent grin
What a wonderful day, for your day to begin.

Your day is busy; you work hard and well
Always happy under Nature's spell
The Sun begins to set; your day's been well spent
You head to bed, happy and content
But the day's glory is not over yet
Just lay there a while, it will happen soon
You fall asleep with a smile on your face
By the fantastic light of the great full Moon.

Nature provides wherever we live
We just have to look and She will always give
People go about without seeing the real picture out there
They concentrate on their stresses
All they need do is stand a while and just stare
In city, town or country, Nature finds a way
To please each and every one of us day, after day, after day.

Fiona Cary

Sonnet To Violets

Oh violets! . . . I never thought that I'd see
A wild flower as elusive as thee
In shades of pale, deep violet, white and
Paler still . . . mysteriously in land
Of my garden grow; in magic woods of
Childhood - with friend - we would gather posies
And homeward wend; over the years 'twould be
A rare sight indeed to see thy shyly
Peeping face; just one lovely thought to light
A sad or lonely time . . . and turn it bright!
Such is the power of thee, sweet flower
As from winter's frost thou spring . . . magically!

So long as this world keeps on turning . . . may
Yearning sad hearts keep thy image always.

Valerie Hall

Nature's Power Unveiled

Crackling thunder and lightning flashes
Torrential rain with deafening crashes
Light so bright that eyes just blink
That run for shelter is all we think
Riverlets of water so quickly forming
Danger! Alert in the mind is dawning
Shelter! Some shelter? This need essential
Battered, soaked to the skin with this torrential rain
No choice but to bear nature's roll curse the elements and blame
But nature's protectnics so quickly diminish
When dark turns to light, creating a different image
Storm clouds pass, fleeing the skies
As moonlight, once more caress the eyes.

Brian Wharmby

Sixth Sense

They look at us and think how sweet,
such animals in a zoo to keep.
They take our photograph
and joke and laugh.
They buy our furs and hide,
and then try to protect us with a logic somewhat cockeyed.
But what these two-legged human freaks do not understand
is that we animals have the upper hand.
In times of danger and disaster
we are known to act much faster,
for, despite all man's technological advance,
to protect him from any mischance,
it is the four-legged and winged beast which possesses the
ultimate defence -
an acutely developed sixth sense.

Peter Schapira

Watching Trees

Here is a small one
Waving wildly
The strong ones - nothing
Some branches are anemones
Others are fingers
The rest but shadows
To hide in
One day I saw them in the daylight
Stand tall
Digress into greyness
Be still with a gentle sadness
And remember they once had leaves.

Demian Reed

The Seasons

Autumn with its glorious colours has arrived
The daylight hours grow shorter every day
When we see birds gathering to fly to warmer shores
We know that winter will soon be on its way.

A time when the land lies desolate and bare
And later on becomes gripped with ice and snow
When icicles hang from the rooftops and the trees
A time when we must be careful as we go.

But we know that this won't last forever
And that spring will soon be on its way
A time when all nature will be reborn
And the hours of daylight growing longer every day.

Spring will be superseded by the summer
A carpet of flowers will grow beneath our feet
The fruit in the orchard will gradually ripen
And the cycle of the seasons is complete.

Ronald Martin

Tsunami Palm

Amidst the rubble and devastation of an Indonesian island,
Ravaged by earthquake and flood,
Stands a solitary palm tree
Tall and erect amongst the debris.
While bodies lie unaccounted for
Under mounds of fallen buildings,
And others have been swept out to a watery mass grave,
And the living wait for aid and news of their loved ones,
The palm remains, tall and proud,
Displaying its crown of leaves -
The same leaves that formed a 'red carpet'
For the King of Kings on his triumphant entry into Jerusalem
The palm tree, tall and stately,
Israel's symbol of victory.

Kathy Rawstron

Spring

When spirits dip in winter's grip
Of darkness cold and rain,
The solstice turns pervading gloom
To thoughts of spring again.

Creeping light curtails the night
Drawing days out longer,
And warmth invades the icy chill
When the sun gets stronger.

Delicate snowdrops fight for life
Each like a pearly tear,
Before bright golden daffodils
Announce that spring is here.

As dormant trees and plants to please
Wake up with buds in bloom,
Their fragrant freshness fills the air
And beauty lifts all gloom.

Returning birds from foreign fields
Just sing and flit and fly,
Whilst building nests in busy haste
For young ones by and by.

New life that's bursting all around
Brings hope for things to come,
Of lazy ways on sunny days
Enjoying summer's hum.

Bill Newham

After Wordsworth

A breeze laughs by and dances daffodils
Fluttering in their beds
The wind screams by and all the daffodils
Are torn to shreds.

Patricia M Smith

Thank You, Sister Earth!

Thank you, Sister Earth!
There are lupines with bright shades!
You have made them real!
Thank you, Sister Earth!
Roses are pink and orange!
You have made them real!
Thank you, Sister Earth!
I see bright purple bluebells!
You have made them real!
Thank you, Sister Earth!
Bright flowers can make rainbows!
You have made them real!
Thank you, Sister Earth!
There are rainbows of tulips!
You have made them real!
Thank you, Sister Earth!
Gerber daisies make rainbows!
You have made them real!
Thank you, Sister Earth!
Bright lilacs are in the snow!
You have made them real!
Thank you, Sister Earth!
Red geraniums are bright!
You have made them real!
Thank you, Sister Earth!
The fireweed is bright purple!
You have made it real!
Thank you, Sister Earth!
The gardens have Christmas lights!
You have made them real!

Laraine Smith

Beyond Planet Earth

I'm standing on this planet
A-looking at the sky
Orion's belt is gleaming
And Sirius nearby.

I love it when the sun goes down
Venus rising as it sets
A beacon in the evening sky -
A sight one can't forget.

I'd like to have a telescope
The kind to see the stars
And galaxies an' planets too
Like Jupiter and Mars.

Sadly, they're too expensive
The ones that see afar
So I'll try to use my human eyes
To seek out every star.

I wish a friendly UFO
Would whisk me off one night
An' take me round the universe
To marvel at the sights.

But I'll have to be content
To stare up at the sky
An' try to figure out 'what's what?'
As the cosmos passes by.

So, 'thank you', God an' planet Earth
For giving us these nights
Without you I would not be here
To see these wondrous sights!

Val Hall

Tsunami Sunrise

Apocalyptic riders coursing by as in a dream
And catastrophic ghastly shapes the saddest ever seen;
The landfall of a homeland, a group of searching souls,
An onward-rushing vision of wild Satanic shoals
Formed from out of Fate's own hand to desecrate the land
In the moistening of demented eyes, so hard to understand.
The dreams of childhood and its goals in ruins now must lie
'Neath idyllic sun and dreamy clouds which arc across the sky;
And swept away forever in an ever-changing scene
Lost generations gone as though they'd never ever been.
And o'er the land our distant eyes watch on, impotent powers
As before the awesome memories of past, the present cowers.
So what then of the future? May be forward cast our eyes
Yet for coming generations 'tis with them the answer lies.
Apocalyptic riders coursing by as in a dream
Have swept away the images of all there's ever been;
Yet images shall be reformed to honour all lost souls
For mankind ceases to exist without such future goals
And the desolate and weary of the sunlit, fate-wrought storm
Shall realise the glory in creation yet unborn.

Ian C Gray

Butterfly Princess

Butterfly princess you flutter with gentleness
You love all the wonderful things that nature provides
You love the breeze that gently guides
You love the flowers' nectar so sweet
Summer's welcoming treat
You flutter in spring's warm sunny skies
As the flowers open their eyes
You flutter as summer puts on her dancing shoes
You love the colourful outstanding views
From butterfly princess to glamour queen
In the summer scene.

Joanna Maria John

Sunshine Days

Power of the sunshine brightens my day
Fluffy white clouds in blue skies arrayed
Temperature rising and birds on the wing
Springtime arriving, a new day begins.

Daffodil stems now pushing through earth
No wonder I'm dancing, it's all this new birth
Stems of the crocus and white purple heads
Tiny white snowdrops awake once again.

Buds on the clematis, climbing the wall
Their lovely pink petals in June, I recall
My red flowering rose, with buds all anew
Gathering in clusters all summer through.

Pansies, so vibrant, with all coloured tops
Heads above rockery, to show off their frocks
Some look like velvet and very serene
Tempting to rabbits to eat if they're seen.

Nature is beautiful and springtime is best
Time when the blackbirds are ready to nest
Hail to the summer and in the bright haze
Spare a few moments to look on and gaze.

Joan Prentice

In The Deep Midwinter

An icy wind, racing snow
Grey clouds, abandoned glow
Shredded trees, withered grass
sunken flowers, river of glass
Punctured time, deep despair
Lack of birdsong across stilted air
Winter's cloak covers all . . .
Thoughts turn to spring and summer's call.

Arthur Pickles

No Kyoto

The leaf fall on the wet field
Cold steels flashing golden light
And sailing quiet autumn bombs
Arrows across our sight
Peeling sheaves of summer
Splendour painted to the night.

In our weather's no prediction now,
Conditions bow and turn,
Seasons broken on our lances
Their entrapment never learned
Till they turn their eyes upon us
Scatter us and burn.
Evening shuts in quicker now
Along with dying light,
Dew skews idols of our time
Sighing quickly into night
And at the last my greedy friend
That's all we ever earned,
At the last my greedy friend
It's all that we deserve,
Served the worst the world
Can pluck in vengeance
From its shelves, elves and demons
In the climes and times
We brought upon ourselves.

Jim Rogerson

Ophelia Of The Swift

Ophelia floats, her flowing mane
Undulates over gravel and grain;
Shoulders covered, then down her back
Waves the moving luxuriant plait.
In Wycliff's Swift thro' mists of time
She lays there nymph becalmed,
Meadow flowers scattered around
Floating with her as she drowns,
I talked to her, she whispered back
In burbling Old English tongue.
Willows askant the glassy brook
Feather-like leaves dipped and shook,
While all around on lea and field
Workers scythed the dusty yield;
Ricks and stooks ranged around
On dry stubble-decked ground,
Farmer checks on Hodge's work
Before returning to his hounds.
Swift still flows its measured way
Then. Now! To the present day. Bank
Steeper now than when I was young,
By degree the river changes shape
Causing tresses to flow a different way
This ancient river thro' mists of time,
Where Ophelia will forever recline.

John L Wigley

Power Of The Plant

A Spaceship lands on Mars.

Nowhere on Earth is there such a scene
Not even in the most fruitful of deserts are plants like these
they encounter ever seen

The first one picks a petal or two and they turn yellow
Bonding to his fingers - like so much adhesive mildew

Acting upon instructions the plant is packed away
Along with other samples, mostly rock, soil, transmitted to Earth
By means of a teleportation - transmission - ray.

After one hour travelling in a mechanised Crick, they came
Upon a lichen-ridden structure made of volcanic brick.
The three Droids took a turn to inspect a notice on the wall
etched thereon in a deeply engraved luminescent scrawl.
This is what they deciphered in Canada; On Earth;
At Space expedition control:

'Welcome Earthmen, welcome to the crypt, home to the plant of life
You are welcome to any part of it - for it is yours now to command;
Understand, why you have come here in the first place looking for
alternate forms of life that might flower and produce a harvest
In your otherwise desolate land'.

The people of Earth were greatly impressed
At last a possible means to feed their undernourished.
Could it be true . . . ?
The message was inscribed by their former ancestors:
Martian colonialists; Previously living on a planet so blue ?

Alan Knott

Winter In The Sun

(Thoughts of retired British 'Snowbird' members of Isla Del Sol Yacht and Country Club in Florida USA preparing for their trip back home to UK following another annual glorious winter in the sun)

How nice it is for us to come
To Florida each wintertime,
For in UK our feet grow numb
With frozen toes, in that cold clime!
So Isla is our second home,
The place where we enjoy to be:
A paradise in which to roam,
So peaceful and at liberty.
For leisure, there are games to play,
Of which, the golf is number one;
While sailors' anchors cast aweigh,
And tennis players catch the sun.
Some play at cards, if they are keen;
We like to dine inside our club,
We tarry at the nineteenth green,
Refresh ourselves inside the pub!
Before we know it, spring is here,
How fast time flies with happiness!
Now we must pack our clothes and gear,
Return back home, to reminisce.
Another winter's come and flown,
But home is home, and will remain
A special place that is our own:
Yet, winter we'll be back again!

Christopher Head

Our Planet Earth

Lift up your eyes to the heavens
Instead of looking down
Look up and be proud of living
With all nature's wonders around
Look at the trees and flowers
Look at the rivers and seas
Look at the mountains and valleys
Look wherever you please.

Who can compete with nature
Or who can fashion the stars
Let us take care of our planet
Or it will become just like Mars
Take a look at the moon way up in the sky
Is this what we want? Must our wonders die?

Explore all of nature, by not just a glance
Think? How did they happen? Not merely by chance
Who made all these wonders? And placed them here?
Why do we waste them? And not hold them dear
And what of our children as they come along
Will they be strangers? Or will they belong?

Pat Adams

The Bora Wind

Out of the east the vandal wind
Marks its destructive spree
By crashing through the ravaged land
Then raging to the sea.

It blows the froth off foamy clouds
And gives the air a thwacking.
It snaps the spines of hunchbacked trees
And sends the pine cones packing.

It turns the tides back out to sea
And agitates the breakers,
Beats fishing boats against the rocks,
Now flotsam widow-makers.

Seagulls in shrieking concert soar,
A phalanx in fast motion.
With urgent flap of wings they fly
Above the boiling ocean.

The Bora's sound can change at will,
A voice without a face.
It hoots and howls, it groans and growls
Then whimpers into space.

Celia Thomas

Skimming

With frilly mane and curling tail
I live an upright life
Though over me great ships may sail
In time of calm or strife
I'm proud of what I am, of course
On obviously *neat* sea horse.

But so hard to be related
To a bit of *seaweed*
Why so crazily created -
- So haphazard, indeed
That its fish species is in doubt
As it floats carelessly about.

Such a tatty-looking surprise
With some bits transparent -
A master of disguise?
Yet it is all too apparent,
Anywhere streaming on and on,
It thinks itself a *sea dragon* . . .

An appearance extravagant
Enough to make you grin
Though some do think it elegant -
Neck and back each a fin -
But most of us think it is coarse
And nothing like a neat sea horse.

People on boats have no notion
Over what they're skimming
Yes, great creatures of the ocean
Like the whales seen swimming
They take note - but not such as we
My seaweedy cousin - and me.

Christine Mary Creedon

A Secret

How privileged was I
In that moment to see him
When he stood proud and alert
With the moon shining down
Listening to every sound
When no human was around.

From the bedroom window
In secret I watched him
In the middle of the road
On the shed roof, across gardens
In his own world, when people were sleeping
It was his domain to do as he wishes
Calling to his mates as he went.

What beauty he beheld as he stood alone
Entranced by the street lamp
A lone soul in the night
From behind bedroom curtains
In secret I watched him.

I will not tell his secret, only I will know
For some people would call him vermin
Others a pest, but there in the moonlight
What beauty he bestowed
How can he be ripped apart in the name of sport?
Hounded by dogs, till his heart gives out.

He may come again, when the moon is full
To stand under the street lamp
When people are sleeping
But his secret is mine
What was it I saw?
It was a handsome dog fox
That man wishes to destroy.

Patricia Plumpton-Edwards

Wild Firebird

Once I spied a wild firebird venture into a tree
I did my best to coax him near
Enchant him to abide with me
So tall and graceful when in flight
So lordly in the sky
More sun cascading off him as he spreads his wings up high.

Then one day as he flew by, he came upon my hand
Trusting, nestled in my palm
As thought on tall tree, leaf or land
I let him dampen his red flame
To stop from burning my pale skin
And away from the glistening daylight rays
The shadows spread in within
Carefully cradled in my gentle grip
His spirit began to ebb away
Frailty that was once beautiful
Had started to decay.

In guilt, unfurling all my grasp
I knelt down at his tree
Tried to return what was taken in love
In taming the wild and the free
Caging the lightning smothered the bird -
Emptiness unable to fly
He nestled into dying roots
And looked up at the sky
And died.

Denise Delaney

It's Just That Sort Of Morning

It's just that sort of morning
Through golden pollen haze
Knee-deep in flower-strewn meadows
When you think of holidays.

It's a marmalade-y morning
With orange juice and toast
On neat clipped lawns for breakfast
Blackbird singing on a post.

It's a tranquil sort of morning
Bees rest in flower heads
With butterflies on noiseless wings
Of yellows, mauves and reds.

It's a scrumptious sort of morning
Marshmallow white cloud dream
A bee-droned scented garden
Near a babbling woodland stream.

It's a madcap spring-like morning
Pretty girls with boys to tease
Chasing hats and swirling skirts
From restless, gusty breeze.

It's an outdoor sort of morning
On moor or Lakeland fell
For hikers, walkers, ramblers
It's like a magic spell.

It's a misty sort of morning
Dewy grasses, silver sheen
A gentle hint from nature
That summer's left the scene.

Peter Colenutt

Springing To Life

Out for a walk in the country one day
I wonder what I'll see along the way?
Down the winding path to the bridge across the brook
What's on the other side? I'll just have to take a look
There, over there, a little fawn sitting under the shade of a tree
Looking up at the blackbirds, one, two, three.
Oh, a butterfly hovering above her head
Such magnificent colours of blue, black and red
Jumping in and out of the hedgerows
Sparrows twittering away, busy collecting to build their nests
Some twigs, fur and bits of hay
It's lovely to walk at this time of the year
Seeing everything that's bursting into life
It's refreshing to leave behind the bustle, stress and strife
Look at the bulbs peeping through the Earth
Daffodils, bluebells, new leaves on the trees
Blossoms of pink, yellow and white gently swaying in the breeze
Over in the tall grass, hopping about a rabbit with her mate
And just behind is the farmer with his prize bull
Just going through the gate
Off down the footpath the sun shining bright
We come across a lake
There's ducks swimming freely, a family of swans
Time for my picnic of tea, sandwiches and cake
Over on the field some dogs playing rough and tumble
                                        on the cool grass
An elderly couple arm in arm, smiling at them as they pass
Children playing, having fun, for a group it's football
Some cricket, others just happy to run.
'It's a goal!' with excitement I heard one of them shout
While mums and dads are lazing, chilling out
Back down the lane on my way home
There's a sight I didn't expect to see
A fox by the hollow of a great oak, standing, staring at me
There is so much to see in the countryside
So remember to always take care
Love and respect the country code
God's creation is for everyone to share.

Mary Ward

The Mountain Rim

Sunset on the western mountain rim
I saw as a beauteous visual hymn
In the crater; periphery of my young life
Enclosed, and free from worldly strife,
we knew a soothing, natural harmony
With eternal hills and captive sea.

The mountain grandeur holds in thrall my heart
And though fate decrees that I must live apart,
These timeless hills, yet beckon me
To their sheer ramparts and the sea.
For their compelling presence I still yearn
And to them my ageing eyes now turn.

Enveloping mists on rugged, green-clad slopes
Made a backdrop for my youthful hopes
And winter storms, their headlong rush denied
Spread their captive rain on the mountainside
In nostalgia, still they haunt my dreams;
Ageless hills and mountain streams.

Patrick Glasson

Orchestrated

Pale sunshine, bereft of warmth
Sinks its pastel held as
Distant thunder clouds chase
Across the bruised purple sky
Clapping faintly the strike of lightning.

Raindrops caress the ground
Crescendo to a heavier beating
Keeping time with intermittent hailstones
Winds whip calm waters into turmoil
Blowing themselves out
Backsucked to nothing
Crashing into headlands.

Beverly Maiden

The Ash Waltz

Waltzing in the wind
Rhythmic co-ordination
Swirling in unison as the wind passes through the valley
Circling red kites dance effortlessly, high above the ash,
                                        racing thermals
Not tethered like the ash
But free to waltz with the wind
Bowing, knowing heads at the coming and goings of our world
Ash bows and bends once more against the turbulent forces
Rain washes leaves and branches making ash as new - beautiful in
                                        greens and browns
Now ash is ready for the waltz again as gusts buffet the valley
Ash stands tall and elegant swaying this way and that way to the tune
                                        of the day

One, two, three, one, two, three
This way and that
The clouds recede, the kites appear, flying against the patchy
                                        azure sky

Ash takes a rest to attend to her attire
Some leaves and twigs have gone
But ash will be ready to dance again.

Hilary Jean Clark

Summer

Summer, oh how I love summer at bay
Out comes my bag, sandwiches, biscuits
Pop, towels, spray,
Screaming, fighting kids all the way
Soon as I hit that beach
So much space at bay
Kids quieten down, fun it is all the way
Happy summer days, thanks to the beach at bay.

Denise McDonald

Talking With Animals

As I was walking 'cross the lea
Through clover smelling free and sweet
A rabbit bounded from my feet
And raced for shelter, way from me.

I reached the verges of the field
With peewits stabbing open land -
They screamed in anger at my stand
To further pastures off they wheeled.

The wood was cooler, greener still
Just insects' hum and crows' rude *Craake!*
I trod with care, no sound to make
And clearly heard woodpecker's drill.

Then, startled fox, whose eyes flashed, *Flee!*
Paused for a heartbeat, tail held low
I posed no danger, but he couldn't know
And so he raced away from me.

Lilian Perriman

Tsunami

The world on its axis is rocked in space
On Earth Tectonic plates rearrange their state
Without a sound beneath the sea
An eruption creating a tsunami
Disaster befalls the innocent race
As the sea claims its victims
Who disappear without trace
Bringing death and destruction
An earthquake unique
Is the hand of 'Satan'
At work in the deep?

Ernest Hannam

Dreaming Of Summer

A nicely chilled Martini
Marilyn in a bikini
Strawberry Cornetto
Ferry led falsetto
Boomed out Roxy tunes
Hold 'em no size zeros
Dancing at Cafe Nero's
By the church fair Reverend Scoons.

A barbecue murmurs
Powell and Pressburgers
At the movies tonight.

A hosepipe bandana
Sun oh how Havana
Over fence rumours
Washing line bloomers
Cast a shadow over us loons
Book ended novellas
Ice cream sellers
Passing flying church fair balloons.

Marc E Wright

Field Gate

I have nails and screws
But hardly used
A friend called stile
I get a shave from a file,
There are hinges and a bracket
Then someone oils my racket
Sometimes I fall asleep
Then opened for cows and sheep,
I have never wanted paint
But Hell this ain't
Frost, snow and rain
It all feels the same,
Me and my friend stile
We get jumped over once in a while
It can get lonely, especially at night
Gazing at the stars and the moonlight,
Even though we are rotten
We will never be forgotten
For every path to take
A stile and gate they will make.

G W Culshaw

The Five Senses

Touch -
Feel the wind on face
The smoothness of velvet
The jagged touch of rocks.

Taste -
Honey-sweet nectar
Sharp saltiness of brine
Curry - hot flavour.

Smell -
The heady Heaven-scent jasmine
The rotting odour, rubbish tipped
Mid the souring scent from sighing pines.

Sight -
Night. Eyes - wide-eyed, watchful
Days. Dawn-fed chorus, struck, yet free
Moles, mound-full, yet managing.

Hearing -
Delicious birdcall, dawn-raised
Later, quiet contentment, full-beaked, featherlight
Booming contrast, boot-laden, youth-spoken
Quintet lucky, five live, full fortune free
Accepted, acceptable - grant taken
So human - we.

Valma June Streatfield

The Four Seasons

The sun's coming out, it's the start of spring
Because the birds outside are starting to sing
Hyacinths and daffodils are ready to bloom
The fragrance of spring soon fills the room
Leaves are appearing upon the trees
Makes a change from the cold winter freeze.

Golden fields of barley and wheat
All set out in rows, all nice and neat
Rare flowers in bloom, ever so bright
Growing wild, what a wondrous sight
Warm winds blow, it's a summer breeze
Can you hear it whisper through the trees?

Nuts and berries in abundance to be found
Trees shed their leaves all over the ground
The bright reds and oranges, colours so bright
Farmers are ploughing well into the night
See how the wind blows through the trees
We're getting ready for the cold winter freeze.

Cold winds blow from the far North Pole
Chilling the bones of both young and old
Snowflakes fall softly, gently covering the ground
Cold winds blow, it's an eerie sound
Keep snug and warm and stay out of the cold
Next year's seasons are ready to unfold.

Susan Kami

Nature

The ethereal mountain dew
Reminds me of everything natural and true
The soil whispers secrets of the soul
Amidst the debris of lost love's toll
The sun permeates the winter frost
Reminding one of childhood dreams now lost
The burning gorse heather
Remind one nature even reached its tether
Like mankind, the land deserved respect
Falling fallow when left to neglect
The trees glisten in the soft summer rain
Like gentle grace it relieved pain
Spring's healing rays
Are there for anyone who prays
And seeks beauty in a higher being
Who created all we are now agreeing.

Finnan Boyle

Spring Clean

My mop was poised above the filthy floor.
Steam from the bucket swirled around my face.
I couldn't stand the muddle any more.
Today was set aside to purge this place.

And then the telephone began to ring.
I tried to leave it, but it summoned me.
A friend suggested celebrating spring
By driving to the coast, to see the sea.

For one brief moment I was racked by doubt.
Temptation won - I think, for friendship's sake.
Changes of plan are what life's all about
And winter-weary souls deserve a break.

Without a backward glance we sped away;
The housework will be there another day.

Jean Hayes

Adventurers' Fen

Drizzle dulls the early summer evening
As the sound of no sound calms the senses
Birdsong clears the mind, as the wind whispers
Through the reeds, mourning days past, days lost.

Suddenly a white ghost swoops
Then hovers, searching, silently plummeting
To Earth before rising; a small mammal
Swinging from sharp talons, heading skyward.

A life given for a life
Held in the sound of silence.

And here, enthralled by the stillness
In the soft embrace of Mother Earth
Safe with the sound of no sound
A quiet peace, a pure joy
And time to recall past loving.

Anita Richards

The Wood

Wood holds wind gently
High branches
Sifting sound like hiss
Falling sand
Light under trees green, yellow
Like bending
Reflections; trees/sunlight
In green water
Fox walks past, reddening
The shadows
Now all is still, nets sunlight
Drift under
Over blue dust air gleams
Vanishes
Wood drowsy at peace, quiet
Afternoon subsides.

Teresa Webster

Sunset

Does the river need the light of day
To find the open sea?
Does the sun its vigil of the Earth
Depend on you or me?
And our presence
Or our absence
Is of little consequence
For seasons know
And all obey, divine intelligence
Will the stars shine any brighter
Or the deserts be no more
Will the loving embrace of the sea
Fail to caress the shore?
And will mankind
On the morrow
A greater wisdom see
When we are gone
And take our leave
Of this humanity.

Windsor Hopkins

Untitled

Mist on fields as sun is rising
My sight is dim but hope's returning
The sun is bright and the light is burning
Into my waking mind
Look into my eyes to find
The sleeper greet the dawn
The mists of night are departing
Into this day I am reborn.

Mark Summers

Autumnal

Swans that fly across our skies
Talk as they fly those graceful birds
Not one, not two, but a flock
A sight to see at autumn time.

Autumnal is the word I seek
That time of year for warmer climates
Little birds that summer here
Must fly south for wintertime.

I wish you safety, upon your flight
Strong wings, that will carry you home
Come back next year little birds
I'll wait till then, my little friends.

Now is the time to see
Different swans upon our shores
They winter here in our land
So regal are these graceful birds.

When seasons come and go
Lives are changed once again
Now we see our world
In shades of yellow, red and brown.

I have the time to sit and stare
This perfect world so beautiful
With birds that fly across our skies
Insurmountable, pleasure given.

I love this land in which we live.

Carole A Cleverdon

May

M aypole dancers
A pple blossom
Y oung lambs frolic.

Joyce Walker

Solent Blue

Clear blue sky not a cloud
Ryde church tower standing proud
Isle of Wight beckoning fair
All revealed in the crystal air
Rolling Downs enhance the view
Bembridge, Cowes, Fishborne too.

Solent seas, calm and tranquil
Seaborne flotsam at a standstill
Ferries crossing at their ease
Triangular sails seek a breeze
Outboard engines cough and splutter
Flags and pennants lazily flutter.

Sea birds rest on the placid sea
Sunbathers bask on the beach at Lee
Sand eel shoals boil the water
Mackerel squads lead the slaughter
East to west the panoramic view
Highlights the beauty of Solent blue.

Peter Smith

Fox

Expert at the soft tiptoe,
champion of speed,
braver of the winter snow,
his hungry cubs to feed,
chief of every glen and glade,
guard of every trail,
shadower of every shade
that flits round hill and vale,
dancing partner to the night,
groom to Dark's sweet bride,
prince of starlight,
star of moonlight,
king of the countryside.

Kate Williams

Cressbrook Dreaming

This land is but a dream
With silent valleys and running streams
With Spirit in the earth around
Heartfelt moments can be found
In weir and brook and hill and peak
Your solitude is what I seek
To give my mind, my heart, my soul
Your wondrous secrets to behold
Who knew I would find such a treasure?
That gives me real earthly pleasure
No other wealth holds such a key
To find joy in eternity
Of nature's gifts of land and sky
And hills and peaks to look up high
I walk, I climb, I run, I dance
My life you definitely enhance
Thank you Cressbrook, thank you land
You hold my heart in your mighty hand
Of hill and tree and brook and stream
I will always dream . . .

Karen Harvey-Zahra

Viewpoint

Looking through the portholes of glass
Framed with grease and dust in equal proportions
Out into the roughly grassed fields
Sprouting snouts of metal bars
And narrow-fronted molars of wooden sheds
Designed more for stray rodents and scarecrow-like sea birds
Than any pretension to human comfort
Across the tarmac nerve centre
Alive with roaring horse-power and bad-tempered drivers
Moth-eaten horses graze near a principality of electrical structures
That trap and twist space up in their curved wires
Like a hairdresser perming a client's hair.

Laurence DE Calvert

A Month In May

I took my camera out
and snapped May time's bloom.
It's turning twilight and I'll be going home soon.
I soaked up the day,
then my dentist appointment came.
The fresh, green, leafy tunnel of emotion,
made me forget about the pain.
I sat in the cafe with Jackie,
and the sun hit my back through the window.
The day is balmy and I feel lazy
I say goodbye after a cafe latte
to quench my thirst.
Bank Holiday comes and I paint the wall
as blue as the sky
It compliments dawn's colour
and I feel nature healing me
I've made my place as fresh as spring
and very Feng Shui.
I never had chance to say goodbye,
for May is over too soon
As we leave spring behind,
it's final merry month and enter summer -
and start with flaming June.

Rachel Van Den Bergen

Early Spring

Early spring
the weather is still cool.
Together, in the garden
so fresh with morning air,
we make a mud model of you
with your stubborn chin
and one of me
with eyes in the shape of
almonds.

But I break the models
into hundreds of pieces,
provoked by I know not what
sometimes my mood swings;
more violent than a tightened
string.

Without a word you gently mix
the broken pieces of us
with water. Your tenderness
surprises me; and once
again you make a model of you
and a model of me.

Now there's me in you,
and you in me.

Tammy Ho Lai-Ming

The Serenity Of Summer

I lie in the long grass and surrender -
Submit willingly
To the warmth of the sun
And the tranquillity and peace all around

Butterflies with fluttering flight
Spread colour everywhere -
The drowsy hum of bees and birdsong
The rustle of leaves in the trees above

A beautiful dragonfly zooms in,
All blue and green and long gauze wings,
Nibbling at a leaf
Before darting off again

This is always summer for me -
Warmth and tranquillity and peace -
Nature's bounty all around
The perfect time for serenity.

Diana Price

Summer Colours

A red-hot sunny day
Children happily at play
Golden beaches, blue seas
Salty air with sea breeze.

Soothing songbirds, azure skies
Watching colourful butterflies
Barefoot walking, holding hands
Digging toes in sun-warmed sand.

Doreen Hampshire

Starry Nights

Starry nights
Where lovers sit and talk
Sandy beaches
Where they walk
Hand in hand across the beach
They hope to reach.

A cloudless sky
They gaze and stare
Only of each other are they aware
Building castles
In the sky
Living for each other -
Never wondering why.

E Jane James

Artistic Colours Of Spring (Acrostic)

S trolling 'round my garden, what a joy it is to see
P rimulas and pansies, as pretty as can be
R osemary, forget-me-knots, bells of deepest blue
I n the blue range, catnip and lilacs blooming too
N eat and sweet the violets, always shy of course
G old forsythia, wallflowers, pale yellow on the gorse

P ink blossom on the cherry, white flowers on the pear
A pple has both colours that it is proud to share
L ush, the many shades of green on grass and shrub and tree
E ach one plays its part and gives delight to me
T he background for the multi-hues of so many coloured flowers
T hat please my eye and soothe my soul as I while away the hours
E njoying the sight of new growth, refreshed by soft spring flowers.

Ida Jones

Cretan Dream

(For Linda Bennett)

The empty crash of foaming surf
Cascades over rocks and sand
Where I sit myself, but not alone
As though Heaven were close at hand.
Behind me across some sunburned turf
Washed by a bladed ceiling fan
She sleeps herself, but not alone
Her voice to me is enough
To melt this meagre mortal man.
To be himself but now not ever so alone
As she sleepily awakes 'neath the turning fan.

John Liberkowski

Summer

Swifts cut the heated air,
tiny black daggers, piercing
the silent water.
The frog's open-mouthed
chorus a balm to
the swollen sun.
Lying on my back,
light bulb-red filters my
fingers and grass tickles
spiders' webs over my skin.
Lazy footsteps bear a
chiming tray, ice sweating
in warm glasses.
The summer's longed for heat
a burden now.
Heavy on mercury bones.
Molten metal hazes a mirage
in the desert.
The world shimmers.

Emma Leech

Transition

From the old into the new
December days bring Christmas near,
With the past year's end in view
And the coming of the New Year.

Christmas draws us to recall
The values that do make for peace;
Goodwill and harmony to all
Which, if fostered, will never cease.

With courage then the future face,
The truths we learn from Christmas Day
Let us with gladness firmly embrace
And practice all along life's way.

We shall a ray of sunshine spread,
Where clouds on many a life hang low
As they life's pathway fearfully tread
And a blessing on them richly bestow.

Stanley Birch

Appeals To My Senses

Shedding winter woollies gives us all such a thrill
Time to try on summer suits, do they fit us still?
I enjoy the various blooms as they appear
Light mornings hear dawn chorus, trill sounds reach my ear.

Out walking each face bears smile of people you meet
Youngsters spend many hours playing in the street
Spot couples strolling, ice creams in the park
Because it takes hours before everything goes dark.

There's nothing bad about summer season to say
I for one, never want it to just fade away
Aches and pains in summer are bearable daily
Even attempt my housework with aplomb gaily.

Susan Mullinger

Summer

Autumn rains
Winter howls
Spring springs
Then
Summer sings.

The summer sun
Wakes you up in a morning
Makes you stay out late at night
Brightens up even the dullest of days.

As
Flowers flourish
Trees prosper
Birds sing
Bees buzz
Children play
People smile
Those at work can't wait to sunbathe.

Barbecues aplenty
Beer flows
Gazebos go up
Umbrellas? Who needs those?

Sadly summer ends
As most good things do
But I look forward to seeing summer again
And so should you.

Anthony Doolan

Light Nights At Last . . .

Lighter nights are here at last
So summer's here, hope it doesn't go too fast,
Sunshine glistening through the trees,
Out come the butterflies and bees -
Strolling through scented flowers
They smell so good after summer showers.
Having a barbecue in the evening light,
The aroma of cooking is such a delight,
Work isn't over for everyone this day
In the fields, strawberry pickers earn their pay.
As the sun moves slowly through the sky,
The temperature cools after being so high,
The pub's still busy, as twilight falls
And in the garden the blackbird calls.
After a drink, to the beach we go
Watching the tide's ebb and flow,
In the distance you can hear the sound
Of amusements and rides going round and round,
The lights on the rides are sparkly bright
Twinkling in the early evening light,
The moon shines down from above,
Making us think of romantic love,
Lovers walk around hand in hand,
Going across the golden sand,
The sea laps gently at their bare feet
The long, light nights are such a treat . . .

Salli Noble

Summertime And Bees

I pause to watch
A bee at work
So busy in his chores
Humming as he flies
From flower
To flower.

Never pausing
His endless work
Never seeming to tire
Humming as he flies
From hour
To hour.

I pause to watch
A bee at work
From my work through the day
Humming along too
Taking time
To take time.

So pause and look
Around yourself
Take some time in the day
Humming your own tune
To lighten
Up your way.

Gillian Jones

Springfield Park

Travel by train
Visit Grandma
And Grandpa
On a sunny day

Leave the tower
Block of flats
Find the oasis
Among the grime

Sailing boats
Across the pond
Higher the swings
Dizzy roundabout

Holding hands
And queuing up
An ice cream cone
A special treat

Grandpa sitting
On the grass
Feeding ducks
With Grandma's bread

Time stood still
In this little haven
On the busy
Streets of London.

Debra Webb

It's here

It's here, it's here, just listen to the cheer
No more freezing mornings
No more freezing nights

The man on the radio he said the magic words
It's the first day of summer, I know I heard those words
No more rainy bus stops, no more freezing fog

We can look forward to bad air quality, thank God hazy smog
Oh yes, it's summer, thank God it's here at last
It just takes so long to come, oh please make it last

Now I am quite excited, hosepipe bans on the way
I am sure I heard him say it, limit your water every day
Oh yes, that's more like it, now I really know it's here

And now I know it's really true
Because at Number 78 she has just strolled into the garden with a
bikini that's not real great, she is 59 if not more
But I know it will only fit the teenager next door

I finally calm myself, I know it's really true
I make for the sun cream, I rub in the goo
I lay in the sun for hours, nearly a day
Oh, I am so scared the sun will go away

I hear another voice bellowing from the radio
He confirms all my dreams, summer is here to stay
Well, at least for a few weeks, before it goes away.

Michael Stephen Vanderpoll

Through The Window

Early, on a summer's morn
I am so glad that I was born
I look out thro' the window glass
To watch the squirrels on the grass!
Birds - all colours, shapes or size
At different times, before my eyes
Sometimes pheasants strut around
Or a fox appears on the ground!
Once a badger came to call
I'm never alone - I've got it all
Not enough hours in the day
For me to tire of watching them play
I eagerly rise, at early dawn
To see their antics, on the lawn
Even days when 'rain stops play'
My feathered friends, don't go away.
They sing their songs from sheltering trees
Or protest loudly in the breeze.
Sometimes, a cat sleeps under the shed
Lazily watching, but he's well fed
Never bothers to chase the birds
He knows if he did, he and I would 'have words'!
He stretches a paw and goes to sleep
More than happy - the peace to keep
My garden is my secret world
Of imagination and Heaven - unfurled!

Evelyn Mary Eagle

Sunrise At Ganpatipule

Rays shine out
Over misty woody hills
Painting the sky a
Pastel pink
Which is then reflected
In the tidal river
A double beauty of the sun
The eternal giver.

He then showed his head
Up above the clouds
Only half out now
But still strong and proud.

Fully out now
In the blink of an eye
Pink gives into yellow
As he lights up the sky.

It's easy to see
How we once worshipped
The sun
Each new day is creation begun.

Benedict Thomas Cox

Gently Touch You

As the summer breeze
Caresses the leaves
On the gently swaying trees
Likewise, I will gently touch you
Then, I will quietly pass on
Without you really knowing
Until I am way out of sight
But, I will be beside you
In the quiet of the night
In thought, in word and deed.

Penny Kirby

Tiny Christmas Baby Boy

Tiny Christmas baby boy
Tiny Christmas baby toys
Sparkly tinsel and Christmas snow
Tiny wishes wrapped in snow
Tiny hands, fingers and toes.

Tiny Christmas wrinkled nose
Tiny Christmas baby clothes
Smallish face with a happy glow
Tiny hands gripping, won't let go!

Tiny Christmas newborn eyes
Tiny Christmas just born smiles
Sleeping soundly winking eyes
Tiny, tiny Christmas eyes.

Tiny Christmas listening ears
Tiny Christmas baby ears
Songs of Happy Christmas joy
Tiny Christmas sounds of cheer.

Tiny Christmassey hugs and kisses
Tiny Christmassey dimply pouts
A small Christmas present from God
Pride and joy of newborn's parents
Big, big, big! Larger than *life!*

Naomi Craster-Chambers

Summer - Tanka

A single blackbird
on the treetop above me
stops me in my tracks;
every crystal note is his
yet the song he sings is mine.

Eileen Caiger Gray

The Winter

The winter is coming from what I can see
The harsh winds and rain are nearly upon me
The air feels so cold, with its frosty bite
I can't tell the difference between day and night.

The birds are flying south, to a warmer place
I watch them fly over me in all of their grace
The snow will soon fall, and the children will play
And soon we will be celebrating Christmas Day.

When Santa will come with his bundle of toys
Presents for the girls and presents for the boys
When people get fat in the space of a week
When the alcohol levels will certainly peak.

Everyone is happy and smiling all the time
There is no need for bitterness, hate or crime
The world will get along through this time of joy
Everybody will celebrate and no one is coy.

No one will be selfish and everyone will share
No one will be thoughtless and people will care
The cold rain is bouncing off of the ground
The gloomy darkness has landed all around.

Hannah Ruston

Santa

The white-rimmed cloak of cherry-red
His boots as dark as a midnight storm in the middle of winter
The tangled beard is the early spring frost, that dusts the grass with
such elegance
That jovial voice booming out heartily
Sending ripples of joy through the crowds that surround him,
'Ho, ho, ho and a Merry Christmas to all.'
Yes, Santa Claus with those bright blue eyes, that smile out at you
Giving you hope and ambition for the future.

Will Dawson

A Snowstorm In April

Setting off on holiday
In April, so you think
It's springtime, lots of daffodils
And not a skating rink.
What's this white stuff falling?
No road's been gritted yet
The cars are sliding everywhere
Breakdowns, accidents, you bet.
A slow drive as the snow swirls
The fast lane inches deep
A gritter in the lay-by
A car lies in a heap
A pretty picture emerging
It's like a Christmas card
The banks and fields now glowing white
It's really snowing hard.
What's happened to the seasons?
Are we sure about the date?
No snow in January, wintertime
We get it three months late!

June Melbourn

Winter's Rite Of Passage

Behold the sun behind your tormented spells
Tormenting the light that shies into night

Breathe thrills into the chills of humanity
Chilling the peace for which mad men fight

Excise the tears that have halted to a frost
On the face of time until the end of your rite

Pass on your absent knowledge and leave it behind
Tormenting the life that shies into night

Mark Woodcock

The Gift

(From Christina Rossetti's poem 'In The Bleak Midwinter')

They came with offerings - home-made cakes, sandwiches
on ivy-clad doilies, marzipan stars.
From a pocket I offered my gift - a slim packet
of chocolate fingers, welcomed by smiling faces
placed reverently cross-shaped on a willow plate.
And I felt ashamed at this
the shabbiest of gifts. It had cost me nothing
but money and a fleeting stop at the corner store.

I swallowed my punch and hot mince pie
made my excuses and left.
Running through the rain I felt a longing
to belong. Yet
I knew *my* heart was promised elsewhere.

Jenny Harrow

Will Open Up

The new year will open up
A pathway to the stars
And if it doesn't
Then I won't go far
And if it does
Then I'll make a wish
But if it doesn't
I'll wax apish
But if it does
I'll be nice to children
But if it doesn't
I'll close the kindergarten
But if it does
I'll feed the poor
But if it doesn't
I'll seal my front door.

Muhammad Khurram Salim

Renaissance

Clouds hung, thick and black
Over my patch of world, today.
The garden was pleased -
It had been parched and sere, yesterday.

In the night, rain had stirred
The hard surface of the lawn
And pitted the borders, beating at the flowers
Till some of their slim stems were shorn.

West winds tore at the trees
Hurling their branches, plucking their leaves,
Trying to bend their trunks,
Plait the twigs and make strange weaves.

When the storm passed
And a pale sun shone down
My garden, refreshed, bloomed
Red, green, blue, brown.

Rainwater fills my water butt, again.
Bees hum in the honeysuckle
Birds sing - everything burgeons
Thanks be to God for the rain.

Joan Evans

My Christmas Wish

I wish Santa would call
I wish the snow would fall
I wish for the one thing I cannot have
I wish for this Christmas not to be sad.

My Christmas wish is just one thing
I wish for mistletoe so we can kiss
I wish for this Christmas to be the best one ever
My Christmas wish is . . .
You and me together!

Steven Hunter-Hanlon

Christmas Day

The twinkling of lights
The sweet smell of pine
The traditional mince pie
And warm mulled wine

The gathering of friends
All chattering with glee
The children peeking
Under the tree

The gifts all wrapped
With ribbons and bows
Whatever's inside?
Nobody knows

The cutlery's polished
The table is laid
The wine is chilled
The dinner is made

All these nice things
Make Christmas Day
So exciting and fun
In every way.

Pamela Holt

A Christmas Prayer

Autumn, it has faded
Into a distant glow
Winter throws her cloak around
Awaiting Christmas snow . . .
Evenings they grow darker
Houses they are lit
Fires crackle in their grates
As people warmly sit . . .
Thoughts turn to festive shopping
Buying gifts and cards
Homes are decorated with
Twinkling lights now by the yard . . .
But this time has a greater meaning
Which you may have all lost sight
For a miracle it happened
Right here on this very night . . .
For somewhere in a far off land
We believe - many years ago
A baby was born in a manger and
Changed the world of which we know . . .
Three Wise Men journeyed to this place
They called it Bethlehem
With frankincense and myrrh and gold
And offered it to *Him* . . .
A bright star lit the sky that night
We celebrate Christmas Day
And the world should always give their thanks
And for our blessings - let us pray.

Anne E Roberts

Summertime Breakfast

The sun burning red
Beyond the horizon
It's now slowing, glowing in the sky
Between the houses' chimney pots
5am, must be still in bed
Five o'clock
A flock of hungry starlings descend
On the roadside turf
To search the grassy verge
And gutters' kerbs.

Parked one behind another
Cars, starlings search under
Between the wheels, wheels, searching for meals
A magpie comes looking for a meal
He's rather partial to roadside kill
Blackbird tugs at a stubborn worm
That will not stretch
Bird struggles to pull it out the earth
Breakfast most important meal of the day
Braces of crows eating man's throw-away.

All I can do is watch
Breakfast on roadside turf
All the different kinds of birds
Eating for all they are worth
Out of a dumped rubbish bag
A brown rat, that will fill my needs
He'll do for me
Don't want a lot
Myself Ira Block
An urban fox.

Bryan G Clarke

The Old Year - And The New

It's dank and dark and dismal
Night-time all day long
Gloomy skies of gloomy greys
Shed little light on earthen shades
No sunshine yellows nor brilliant reds
Of summer displays in garden beds.

Dying, dying, dying - gone!
Winter has come
The old year is nearly done.

Yet there is a glimpse of brightness
Robin Redbreast has arrived
And flitting in and out of trees
Are the blues and yellows of busy tits
Blackbirds beaks are yellow
Starlings have their jewelled coats
Jenny Wren's warm, soft, lovely browns
Contrast with finches brilliant crowns.

Evergreens have their berries
Mahonias, their yellow sprays
And rising out of brilliant greens
Are ivy orbs of juicy fruits.

And underground, what work abounds!

Young folk are not hampered
By winter's gloomy greys
Old age has its problems
On dark and dismal days.

But I keep my hope in life a-burning
Of cheer, I have great store
I'll welcome New Year's open door
At my age of eighty-four!

Agnes Hickling

Flower

Bricks and mortar:
Glass panes
Of all shapes and sizes
Soaring and cascading
In myriad colours.

Flourishing scape;
No green
Just reds
Browns and whites
Given the heat
Of light.

A bright star
Up above.

Crimson vistas
Transcending cells
Within.

Youzi Yosypov

The End

It is very white
At the end
An attempted night
A sort of year
What sort of year?
A light dusting
And nothing else
To look at
But the finishing touch
And as such
The final decoration.

Nicola Barnes

Winter's Rainbow

The lilac hues of the pre-dawn
As subtle grey to the
Quiet day
Arise and give your warmth
With sumptuous rays.
See as the chorus rises
Low herald sing (blackbird calls)
A robin's trill
Building as the greyish-green
Turns amber gold with your
Sweet rays.
Adorn with your (gaze)
Radiant glow
No longer linger in those
Dark nights
Awake the dawn
In splendour unadorned
The majesty
Unkempt
With many hues
That you do choose
In colours you adorn.

Jim Breare

Spring

We cannot match her beauty
We cannot capture her grace
We cannot evade our duty
To respect spring's time and place

Spring will return when winter is gone
Each season has its rest
Resplendent in beauty, as in days bygone
The world, once again, is blest!

Joan Thompson

Island Of Dreams

High in the sky, my eyes were captivated by land
Land which held a magical scene one might even say, wonderland
Islands of green, enthusiasm to descend a wealth of creativity
Engulfs the imagination's vision, with considerable mystical dignity

These beautiful *islands* are in a class of their own
A tranquil peace, a calmness, *Nature's* glory so richly shown
Weather elements often have their own determined ways
Patience, the byword excitement, instigates a spectacular display

Each *island* has an atmosphere to relate to its own habitat
Its wildness, its solitude, its welcoming assurance, following the format
The scenery is beyond belief, the ocean roars, but oftime smiles
Reflecting historic values, shipwreck disasters, museum files

Nature has a way with her, reserving something special
Creation of great beauty, a golden flower its essence so gentle
Fields of golden flowers, that dance with distinction sublime
Blending and growing, cultivated with care, in a habitat refined

The Isles of Scilly, so beautiful and serene
Captures the magic of *Nature,* in all its routine
The flowers of gold speak, for all elements, a reference
Spiritually blessed, a decided preference.

Lorna Tippett

Remembering Chotu

Is it *really* thirty-six months today, already, since you left, dearest
Chotu?
It makes me wonder how Father Time toys with our lifespans
I can still recall, it was on the eve of Christmas Eve
How relaxed and happy I was, coming home from work, thinking
My Christmas holidays have arrived! But alas, on that very night
On Thursday 23rd December at 11.35pm, it was to be your final fit.
And on this foggy Sunday late afternoon on 23rd December
I stare outdoors at the fern plant carrying your name and in it
As it moves gently with the breeze, I can see you staring back at me.

Rajeev Bhargava

The Oceans

Seven tenths of the world they rule
Sometimes kind and sometimes cruel
With waters warm and waters cold
Our destinies are theirs to hold.
But when El Nino calls the change
The oceans' currents rearrange
Cold conveyors bringing life
Reverse into death and strife.

White-crested waves still curl the blue
With rising walls, translucent hue
Sapphire mantle fringed with white
Ambition knows not of its plight
Boisterously freed white horses play
Amid the surf and foaming spray
With rhythmic beat they pound the shore
Innocent of the change in store.

Man has no say with currents' role
Though other dangers he can control.
Waves which cleanse the golden sand
And tend the fringes of the land
Leave only tokens from the deep
The varied shells we love to keep.
Now litter lies along the shore
From Man, more wanton than before.

Oil and effluents float as scum
Plastic and debris harms have done.
It's time to wake and realise
We cannot watch the seas' demise
A partnership of Gaia and Man
Should now be our compelling plan
So much to save, so much to lose
We have the options and must choose.

H D Hensman

The Night The Star Was Bright

On a hill far away, shepherds sat to pray
They saw a star shining bright
Knew they had to go on their way
The star was to be their guiding light.

Three Kings together sat to talk
They saw a star shining bright
Talked about the gifts they had sought
Frankincense, myrrh and gold were gifts to delight.

Mary and Joseph sat watching their sleeping child
They saw a star shining bright
Knowing their child was tiny, meek and mild
And that this was a special night.

Carol Paxton

A Cake Of Many Flavours

Christmas is a buckle that holds the old and the new together
Past and future a time too of restoration
God and Man, what is and what could have been
Odours - sounds - sights, fears and hopes
The halls of memory decked with evergreens
Pagan and Christian, spices on the air drifting - hanging
A buckle that fastens reality and fantasy
A season of laughter and tears
Different reality, different expectations
Giving and receiving, wanted and the unwanted
Whatever your wish, season's greetings - my friend.

Clive Cornwall

Forward Press Information

We hope you have enjoyed reading this book - and that you will continue to enjoy it in the coming years.

If you like reading and writing poetry drop us a line, or give us a call, and we'll send you a free information pack.

Alternatively if you would like to order further copies of this book or any of our other titles, then please give us a call or log onto our website at www.forwardpress.co.uk

Forward Press Ltd. Information
Remus House
Coltsfoot Drive
Peterborough
PE2 9JX

(01733) 890099